STILL WINNING

★ ★

Dr. Pontuso —

This is All your
fault. You taught
me how to think & write
about politics.

Most warmly, Chr—

★ ★

STILL WINNING

★ ★

WHY AMERICA WENT ALL IN ON DONALD TRUMP—AND WHY WE MUST DO IT AGAIN

CHARLES HURT

CENTER
STREET®

NEW YORK NASHVILLE

Center Street
Hachette Book Group
1290 Avenue of the Americas, New York, NY 10104
centerstreet.com
twitter.com/centerstreet

First Edition: July 2019

Center Street is a division of Hachette Book Group, Inc. The Center Street name and logo are trademarks of Hachette Book Group, Inc.

The publisher is not responsible for websites (or their content) that are not owned by the publisher.

The Hachette Speakers Bureau provides a wide range of authors for speaking events. To find out more, go to www.HachetteSpeakersBureau.com or call (866) 376-6591.

Print book interior design by Timothy J. Shaner, NightandDayDesign.biz

Library of Congress Cataloging-in-Publication Data has been applied for.

ISBNs: 978-1-5460-7663-6 (hardcover), 978-1-5460-7661-2 (ebook)

Printed in the United States of America

LSC-C

10 9 8 7 6 5 4 3 2 1

To people who work, who
made America great.

CONTENTS

★ ★

STILL WINNING

★ ★

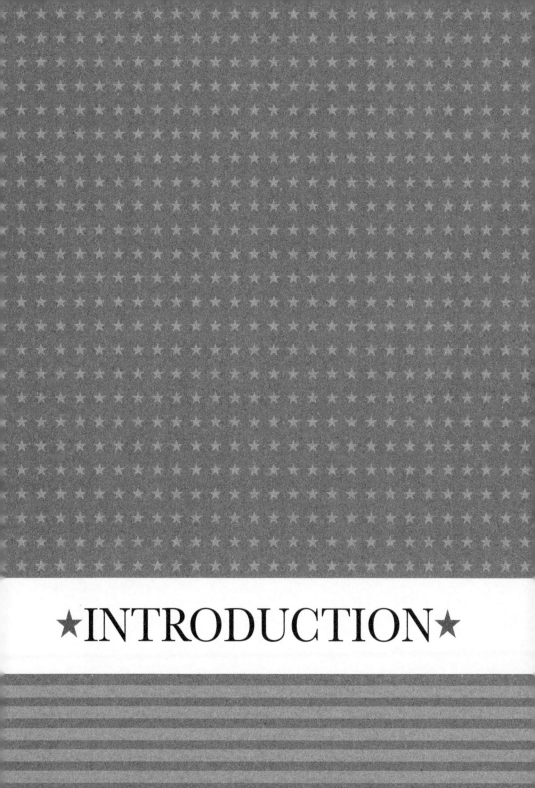

★INTRODUCTION★

DONALD TRUMP

THE NUCLEAR OPTION

This is the story of the unlikeliest of heroes emerging from the unlikeliest of places to take up the impossible cause of an almost forgotten people. They are people who love their country, trust their higher God, obey laws, and will do anything for their family and neighbors. Among them are farmers, factory workers, military veterans, police officers, small contractors, truck drivers, stay-at-home moms, and retirees. They believe in an America founded on bedrock principles aimed at guaranteeing freedom and justice for all. They understand that America is not perfect and never has been, but they believe those founding principles ensure we are always working toward an ideal of fairness, striving for equal justice under the law, and always humble before God. These Americans are not racist. They are not stupid. They are not backward. Some of them have not gone to college but are well-schooled in the basic American ways of hard work, duty, and compassion.

It is fair to say that these citizens are the moral as well as the lineal descendants the Founders dreamed of when they

President Trump boards Air Force One (Official White House Photo by Tia Dufour)

1

hatched the radical idea of replacing a despotic monarchy with self-governance. It would take a special people to grasp and hold this startling concept that man's rights come directly from God—not from a king, not from a government, and certainly not from the corrupt kleptocracy that our government has become. These are the very people the Founders believed could be trusted to make all the decisions about who should lead a free and just government—a government strictly limited in both power and reach.

Who are these people? No characteristic defines them more than this: They are people who work. They work for a living. They work to eat. They work to support their families. They work two jobs, three jobs, maybe four jobs—whatever it takes. They work when they get off work to make life better for themselves and their families. To improve their homes. To improve their land and property. They work to help a friend who is trying to start a small business. Many work so long and hard that they start their own small businesses, and then they hire other people who work. They are people who volunteer. They are people who are the first to open their wallets and pocketbooks when a catastrophe strikes. And if the trouble is close enough, they are the first to show up with their pickup trucks or their boats or their chain saws or whatever they have that might help a neighbor in need.

It is a given among these people that America is exceptional in its compassion as well as its power. They understand that military might is the key to protecting our constitution and our freedoms against the cesspools of barbarians throughout the world. They are cheered by those posters showing a warship teeming with fighter jets, with the words "100,000 Tons of

Diplomacy." They believe in borders because they love America and want to live in America. Not Canada. And not Mexico. They believe America is smiled upon by God, in return for our commitment to freedom, fairness, and equality.

This is also the story of a Leviathan government—the most powerful force in the history of mankind—that has become dangerously unmoored from the people it represents. From the people for whom that government is supposed to work. It is the story of how elites and the politically comfortable who control both parties in Washington seem to be in another world, insulated from reality. In their smug arrogance and hostile indifference, these "leaders" don't even realize how much the people they are supposed to represent despise this uncontrollable monster they have spawned along the Potomac.

So, after more than a generation of relentless despair over the mess in Washington, where could faithful Americans turn? Betrayed at every juncture by all breeds of political swamp rats, was it all hopeless? Or was there a promising glimmer just over the horizon? Or could there be, as my dear mother would ask, reaching for the book of Esther, a leader "for just such a time as this"?

THE MAN WHO WOULD BE PRESIDENT

When Donald Trump descended the glass escalator of Trump Tower on June 16, 2015, much of America was amused that this sultan of brashness and pomposity would have the gall to offer himself as a viable candidate for the presidency. Most of the American political establishment—along with their handmaidens in the media—treated the prospect as an aberration perhaps worthy of a footnote in the annals of political history. But the Donald made good copy, often irresistible copy, as it slowly became clear that this flamboyant and deeply narcissistic businessman and entertainer was deadly serious. But that did not breed respect among many; it only served to stoke an irrational hatred of the man and a determination to stomp out the little fires of loyalty that were starting to pop up.

An almost visceral contempt set in among the media as well as virtually every established politician. They harshly denounced Trump for his message about illegal immigration, unfair trade with China, radical Islamic terrorism, and coddling enemies like Iran. He was branded as a racist, a xenophobe, an isolationist, and as a dangerous, violence-inciting war-monger. Never in modern political history has the media establishment, across the entire political spectrum, fallen into such unquestioning, total lockstep agreement. Left wing, right wing, all around town, almost every media mouth denounced Donald Trump as a reckless demagogue hell-bent on shredding the Constitution and becoming some kind of dictator.

"Now you may have noticed that I have not yet included Donald Trump in our coverage of the Republican presidential campaign this season, and that is because he is obviously never going to be president," said MSNBC host Lawrence O'Donnell a day ahead of Trump's intended announcement.

"Donald Trump will never be president. He knows that. We know that," said then–*Washington Post* writer Chris Cillizza in a column on June 16, 2015. "But his candidacy ensures that for the next several months (at least), he will suck the attention and oxygen away from the men and women who might be. That's great entertainment. But it's terrible for politics."

All pretense of fair journalistic standards vanished. Reports presented as investigative journalism were often go-for-the-jugular attacks. To be sure, of course, Trump's long and unorthodox run as a womanizer and cutthroat business mogul yielded ample derogatory material. What was consistently left out of any equation was the man's uncanny ability to always go for the soft spot, to come up with the perfect description for making almost anyone understand his position.

Indeed, what so many could not see was that this man, so skilled in all sorts of rare arts as a playboy and as a business tycoon was, in reality and most of all, a master of communication. And *communication* was supposed to be the purview of the *media*. But they just couldn't get it. They just could not imagine that someone so rough around the edges, someone capable of such low crudity, someone who was so studiously undiplomatic, was in reality a superb *communicator*—and one, it turned out, who was better at it than all of them put together.

Many of the media's claims were fantastical yet some of their allegations became gospel, even among reporters I had found over the years to be fair and balanced. Some of those friends and acquaintances would soon stop talking to me because I declined to buy in to all the crackpot theories and hysterical claims about how Donald Trump was the second coming of Adolf Hitler or how he secretly wanted to hand the country over to a bunch of Russian oligarchs. His growing base of supporters endured any crazy accusation anybody could come up with—just so long as it might destroy Trump.

"This is racist crap, of course, and to me it's the biggest original sin of Donald Trump," MSNBC host Chris Matthews said in September 2015. Matthews had blasted Trump on his birther claims regarding President Obama. "Before he went after people from Mexico as rapists, which was outrageous. Long before that, he said our president was an illegal immigrant. He played that card and he's still playing it."

"It's not even a race between ideologies anymore," said HBO host Bill Maher in October 2016. "It's not Republican and Democrat or conservative and liberal. It's reality versus alternative reality."

"So much of what Trump says on the stump seems improvised and inconsistent," wrote NPR's Mara Liasson in September 2015. "And on the surface he can look like nothing more than a bombastic showman. But Trump fits right in to the classic tradition of American populism. From William Jennings Bryan to Huey Long to George Wallace to Ross Perot, American populism has always combined nativism with economic grievance."

The most unhinged reporters and writers were not the crazy leftists or even the Never-Trump conservatives like Bill Kristol, founder and editor of the now-cratered *Weekly Standard*. (To be fair, some conservatives justifiably objected to Trump on principled grounds of conservatism.) Rather, the most rabid anti-Trump diatribes came from the middle-of-the-road, studiously nonpartisan journalists who had covered Washington for a long time through Democrat and Republican power without ever showing their hand. They turned out to be the true Swamp Loyalists, the ones who struggled the hardest to protect the system at any cost from a monstrous disrupter like Donald Trump.

In the era of Trump—from the day of his ride down the escalator and then upward to the successful pinnacles of his presidency—no criticism was off-limits. The media openly mocked his looks, ridiculed his private business accomplishments, pilloried his family and children, and made fun of his elegant foreign-born wife—for her accent! On top of all this ridicule and hatred, there was the smug certainty that under no circumstances could Donald Trump get the Republican nomination—much less win the presidency. And once he had made mincemeat of this skepticism, the squalling crybabies in the media mob seemed more committed than ever to denigrating him as a racist moron and destroying him.

Among conservative media, Trump was mocked and ridiculed and worse. The vaunted conservative *National Review* magazine dedicated an entire issue to conservatives of every stripe denouncing Trump. Among the only conservative heavyweights to understand Trump and his supporters early on was radio legend Michael Savage, whose philosophy about "Borders, Language, and Culture" was a blueprint for Trump's campaign.

Through My Own Eyes

Now, a little background. In addition to being a Fox News contributor, I write a column for the *Washington Times* called "Nuclear Option." Its name is in homage to an "On Language" column written by the late conservative icon William Safire. His column appeared in 2005 in the *New York Times* Sunday magazine back when the *Times* was not afraid to allow a brilliant conservative to write for its opinion pages as well as its Sunday magazine. This particular column appeared at the height of the rancorous debate over then-president George W. Bush's judicial nominations.

While history will never forget what Democrats did to Supreme Court justice Brett Kavanaugh after President Trump nominated him in 2018, that was just one battle—the nastiest—in a much longer war. That war began in earnest some fifteen years earlier, after Democrats concluded that the only way to get their crazy and unpopular policies into "law" was by hijacking the federal court system and using the courts to create laws so unpopular that they would never pass in an elected body like Congress. Part of the hijacking involved systematically blocking Bush's nominees for no reason except that the nominees did not buy in to the Democrats' wacky brand of left-wing judicial activism.

Every week Safire's column delved into language and how it was being used, often in the political realm. In this particular column, Safire explained the origin of the term "nuclear option," a secret new parliamentary strategy that was being bandied about in those days as a way to blow past the Democrat minority's filibusters against Bush's federal court nominees.

The strategy was deemed "nuclear" because it was the option of last resort. All other possible avenues for addressing the situation had been exhausted and the filibusters remained. Pulling the trigger on that nuclear option meant total annihilation of the enemy. Maximalist damage. Ultimate ruin.

It was also referred to as the "nuclear option" because of the massive fallout that would plague the United States Senate for years and years after it had been deployed. In a decorum-bound place like the Senate, such brute, heavy-handed tactics are nearly unheard-of. But so were—at that time—the Democrat filibusters that could effectively derail judicial nominations. Ultimately, it was predicted, the "nuclear option" would burn the place to the ground.

At the time, I was a reporter covering judicial nominations for the *Washington Times*. It was an invigorating beat because it was then, as it is now, the place where the most high-minded political philosophy meets raw, street-level partisan politics.

One of the more appalling stories during that time was when Democrat staffers for the Senate Judiciary Committee were caught openly discussing in memos their determination to prevent President Bush from nominating Miguel Estrada—a rising legal star at the time—to the U.S. Court of Appeals for the D.C. Circuit. Among their reasons, they said, "he is Latino." In the memos—which were leaked to me—staffers fretted that if Estrada made it to the federal circuit court, he would be Bush's natural next choice for the Supreme Court.

Democrats would stop at nothing—even outright racism— to prevent Bush from getting credit for nominating the first Hispanic to the United States Supreme Court.

I wrote countless stories about the scandal. Needless to say, most in the so-called mainstream press of the day completely ignored the explosive stories. Still, I took enormous pride in plowing as much new ground as I could.

One lazy recess afternoon when most of the Senate had cleared out, I ran into Senator Trent Lott, the Mississippi Republican who had been majority leader until the press hounded him from office for saying nice things about a ninety-eight-year-old colleague, Senator Strom Thurmond, the South Carolina Republican who had once run for president as a Dixiecrat.

Senator Lott was one of the great masters of parliamentary Senate intrigue. I buttonholed him and asked whether there were any fresh ideas about what Republicans might do to break the Democrat filibusters of Bush's judicial nominees. Indeed, Lott said, there was a supersecret, highly explosive strategy for doing just that. "I'm sorry I can't explain it right now," he said.

I badgered him lightly but all he would say about it was that it would be regarded as "nuclear."

I worked just that much into my story and was delighted when, a few days later, William Safire reported: "Charles Hurt of the *Washington Times* wrote that Lott told him of a plan that might allow Republicans to confirm a judge with a simple 51-vote majority—rather than the 60 votes needed under present rules to 'break' a filibuster. Lott 'declined to elaborate, warning that his idea is 'nuclear.'"

Later in that column—a weekly feature in the *New York Times Magazine* about language—Safire recalled working as a staffer in the Nixon administration. Tasked with presenting the boss with a range of options for resolving a particular dilemma, staffers would couch their preferred option as the centrist one in the middle, sandwiched between feckless retreat and the all-out "nuclear option."

"You submit a memo presenting a range of five choices: the top one amounts to Abject Surrender and the bottom one to Nuclear Strike," Safire wrote. "In this way, the chief executive is induced to choose the one in the middle—Option 3, the most sensible, or at least most centrist, choice."

Safire went on to recall one time when he tried the nuclear option—or Option 3—trick on President Nixon, but someone called his bluff: "I tried to get away with the Option 3 trick once with President Nixon, but his chief of staff, Bob Haldeman, intercepted my decision memo and panicked me by musing, 'Interesting you should bring up the nuclear option.'"

Indeed. Interesting someone should bring up the nuclear option.

———————

HOMEGROWN DEPLORABLE

A little background is in order to shed some light on why I see things as I do. And why in 2015 Donald Trump was in my view the perfect political answer to everything that was wrong in Washington.

For most of my life, all I ever wanted was to write for newspapers. My brother and sister and I started our first single-sheet newspaper when I was eleven years old. Put simply, I liked finding out what was going on and telling others what I found out; if it had a sting to it, all the better. In college, where I majored in political philosophy and English, I worked for daily newspapers every summer and never wanted to go back to school in the fall.

After working at a couple of newspapers in my home state of Virginia, I got a reporting job as an intern with the esteemed *St. Louis Post-Dispatch*, with its storied history in the Pulitzer family. Additionally, two of my favorite correspondents—Ernest Hemingway and Truman Capote—had given me a taste of the American heartland outside of the rural South and I wanted to see it for myself. Soon after, I got my first full-time newspaper job in Detroit, when the *Detroit News* went on strike. After six years in the Motor City, covering murder, the mob, and all manner of mayhem, I got my first job covering politics in Washington. Along with our newborn infant, my wife and I moved east ten days after September 11, 2001.

In my first days in Washington as a political reporter, following the 9/11 terror attacks on New York City and the Pentagon, it was unnerving to see Humvees parked on bridges and at every intersection. Huge military convoys circled the

Pentagon and seeing them on civilian highways around a modern American city was jarring. At the same time, it was also a moment of near-total political unity. The motives and interests of an entire nation were laser focused on a barbaric common enemy that wanted to obliterate every one of us and erase our way of life.

Even as months turned to years and the Bush administration laid out plans for invading Iraq, there was a remarkably united front in Washington. Democrats joined Republicans to green-light Bush's invasion plans. Then-senator John Edwards called Saddam Hussein a "clear and present danger" and "imminent threat." Senator John Kerry, who would soon flip-flop and run a presidential campaign against the war, voted in 2002 to invade Iraq "to disarm Saddam Hussein because I believe that a deadly arsenal of weapons of mass destruction in his hands is a real and grave threat to our security." Former first lady and then-senator Hillary Clinton offered similarly stark warnings. "He has also given aid, comfort, and sanctuary to terrorists, including al Qaeda members," she said. "It is clear, however, that if left unchecked, Saddam Hussein will continue to increase his capacity to wage biological and chemical warfare and will keep trying to develop nuclear weapons."

Clearly, the political class in Washington was unified. Saddam Hussein might not have been directly responsible for the 9/11 attacks, but leaders in both parties were in lockstep that he and his rogue country posed a pressing and legitimate threat to the United States—a threat that could no longer be ignored in a post-9/11 world.

But humming along under the surface of this apparent unity were the same old divisions that separated those who believed in limited government and those who wanted the government to be all things to all people. Though the federal debt was less than $6 trillion at that point, all signs were pointing to the upward explosion that, in fact, came to pass.

Never in the history of the world had a more powerful and far-reaching government been assembled. Yet, increasingly, this government had grown less and less answerable to the innocent citizens. The federal bloat was such that whole departments—vast bureaucracies wasting hundreds of billions of dollars—could be eliminated without any real impact on the average taxpayer. It was maddening to behold, and it fed the national anger over a government gone berserk.

Entitlement spending back then was spiraling toward bankruptcy, although some argued there was still time to fix things before they became dire. Partisans on both sides agreed changes had to be made to ensure the long-term solvency of Social Security, Medicare, and Medicaid. At least there seemed to be a mature recognition on both sides for the need to fix our grave and potentially crippling problems before they consumed us.

The first sign to me of what lay ahead was how quickly the unity behind the Iraq War crumbled. Not because things got ugly in Iraq—all war is ugly—but rather because the next election cycle was fast upon us and politicians were doing the smooth-shoe to abandon any principle that had become inconvenient. For Democrat presidential nominee John Kerry and his running mate, John Edwards, their commitment to the troops they had voted to send into battle lasted only until it became politically expedient for them to turn tail and run.

Think about that for a minute. Kerry and Edwards both argued for the war in Iraq. Both voted to send in brave and heroic Americans to overthrow Saddam Hussein. Not two years later, these two perverted scoundrels were running for the White House on a campaign explicitly opposed to the war in Iraq.

Republicans were not a whole lot better. They were supposed to be the "conservative" party most concerned about the fiscal viability of America's entitlement programs. Around the edges they nibbled to make reforms. And the first chance they got to score a big victory before the next election, Republicans introduced and passed the largest expansion ever of any American entitlement program, known as Medicare Part D.

Meanwhile, federal debt under the supposedly conservative Bush administration climbed from less than $6 trillion to above $10 trillion.

Then came eight years under President Obama, the insufferable merchant of false hope. He had run a thrillingly positive campaign in 2008, then proceeded to govern like a corrupt Chicago alderman, weaponizing the IRS and the Department of Justice and politicizing everything he touched. He turned the cops into bad guys. He went to Egypt and apologized for America's oppression of countries and their people around the world. It was simply mind-boggling to watch—and insulting to any true believers in our Constitution.

Under Obama, the Democrat Party's embrace of "identity politics" reached a fevered pitch. Their political playbook of racial division was no longer a thing of secret memos between Democrats on the Senate Judiciary Committee. The party as a whole came to embrace out-and-out racial political warfare— and what that amounted to was the most highly synchronized display of pure racism the country has ever seen.

Meanwhile, over in the spending department, President

Obama would rack up an additional $10 trillion, boosting the national debt to a whopping $21 trillion for our children and their children to grapple with.

Even as Republicans gained more and more power in the U.S. Congress during the Obama nightmare, they seemed increasingly incapable of delivering on promises. An innocent citizen would be forgiven for thinking that maybe neither side wanted to fix the big problems of our day, because if those problems got solved in a reasonable way, what issues would politicians run on? How would they possibly raise so much money?

Meanwhile, the government continued to become larger and larger—and more unwieldy, more untamable, and more indifferent to the wishes of voters. It was literally a Ponzi scheme where new recruits were desperately needed to keep the payments going to the early investors or else the whole thing would come crashing down.

Interesting that someone would mention the nuclear option.

The 2016 presidential election season dawned with two dozen Republicans clamoring for the nomination. There were conservatives and moderates and libertarians and social preachers. We had had a taste of them all—and all had disappointed.

But oddly, there was a curious element of agreement in this chaotic landscape. We had endured Democrats, conservatives, Republicans, progressives, the Tea Party, triangulators, and even the Contract with America. One thing they all seemed to agree upon was that immigration—legal as well as illegal—was just fine. Those new Americans would be the source for the needed recruits to keep the Ponzi scheme going!

Thus, the last thing any of these operators wanted was a serious, coherent immigration policy. Why? Because it was too hard to tackle and both sides benefited from the broken system. Liberals wanted illegal immigrants to flow into the country, adding to their political base and making the politicians appear to be openhearted and generous. And the Republicans didn't want to seem like they were cracking down on those already in tough circumstances. Then you have the Chamber of Commerce wing of the Republican Party, which represents business owners who benefit from cheap labor without the benefit of a system to determine whether workers are in the country legally.

Also, some in both parties benefited from the cheap labor of illegal immigrants. They want nannies and yard work done for cheap. They benefit from having a permanent underclass of poor workers "hiding in the shadows." Any discussion of this broken issue would be difficult. And Washington doesn't do difficult. So, rather than have the debate they should have had, they just didn't—until Trump forced them.

It was all somewhat liberating for me. By then I had given up trying to report political news as a reporter and had begun writing my "Nuclear Option" column. As much of a relief as it was to no longer have to treat Democrats as serious people, it was also a relief to give up on the Republican Party.

"Throw them all out!" became good enough for me. Just blow the whole damned thing up. Whatever is presidential, let's try the opposite. Whatever is diplomatic, let's try the opposite. Whatever these people in Washington find most horrifying, let's try that.

Needless to say, June 16, 2015, was one of those rare, cloud-clearing days. I will always remember because it was the first time—after fifteen years of covering politics and nearly two decades in the newspaper business—that I ever publicly endorsed anyone for any political office. One minute into Donald Trump's announcement speech, I realized that we at last had a leader "for just such a time as this." It was thrilling, and I endorsed Donald Trump completely, freely, and enthusiastically. Warts and all. He was just what so many had been waiting for and praying for.

In my endorsement column, which I include in the back of the book, I wrote about the heart of why Trump appealed to me and what I now see as his greatest appeal to Americans. He is simplistic in his approach, uncalculated in his remarks, and clear and forceful in what he's offering. The launch of his presidential ambition showed just what I described in my endorsement:

> As presidential announcements go, it was brilliant. It was simple, and it was patriotic.
>
> No sun-splashed park with throngs of rented people jammed around an H-shaped stage. No fake columns.
>
> Just a stage and a velvet blue curtain and a podium. Flanked by American flags carefully folded to show both stars and stripes, Mr. Trump wore a simple uniform of red tie, white shirt, blue suit. Red, white, and blue.
>
> Get it? Red, white, and blue? America's colors? The flag? In other words, Mr. Trump loves America. Get it?

And Trump was never better than when he got down to the nitty-gritty of what's wrong:

If the president and his party are telling the truth about all the wonderful ways government can make your life so much better, why is there rioting in Missouri and Baltimore and California after SIX YEARS of Obama and Democrat rule? Why are so many people so desperately miserable today?

"We don't have victories," Mr. Trump said, before running through all the foreign countries that beat America all the time in trade, immigration, defense and economy.

"I beat China all the time." he said flatly. "All the time."

"When was the last time you saw a Chevrolet in Tokyo? It doesn't exist."

And then the show began.

Through all the tumult and turmoil and political missteps, the scandalously hilarious episodes, my enthusiasm for Donald Trump never wavered in the slightest. More than anything, I never once doubted that he could win, publicly predicting on a daily basis that, in fact, he would win. There have been times when he attacked someone more viciously than I liked. He has issued some outrageous "tweets." He has wandered further from the precise truth than I would have liked.

But for every example of ill-considered comments or behavior, I can point to countless examples of widely accepted, "centrist" establishment politicians who have done the exact same thing. I can give you far more calamitous examples where Americans paid a far more grievous price. Whatever his flaws, Donald Trump is the most accomplishment-driven politician I have ever covered. (Granted, the bar is pretty low in this department.) The press may hate him, but Donald Trump is the most transparent president since the invention of electricity.

The day after I endorsed Trump for president in my column, he began calling me. He is such a courtly and charming and funny guy. He would call under the auspices of wanting advice. But truth is, his instincts were dead-on from day one. I think he really just called because he likes people who like him. And he had hit the jackpot with me. People in Washington are so obsessed with style. And they hated Trump's style. They became blinded with hatred—usually over his style. All I can think of is, if they hate a billionaire real estate mogul from New York City because of his style, can you imagine how much these supercilious folks despise the average American for the same reason?

On these calls, Trump and I would talk politics and policies and gossip. He understood immigration better than any politician I had ever talked to. I suggested that he spend some time understanding gun politics from the standpoint of a regular citizen—who doesn't have bodyguards. The more we spoke, the more I realized that just maybe he really was curious about what I was thinking. Contrary to the media's popular slander that he doesn't listen, he clearly has a finely attuned ear for gathering facts and ideas. For sure, he is quick to dismiss ideas he thinks are without merit, but that shouldn't be seen as not listening. He listens more carefully than any politician I have ever been around.

When we talked early on about the crackling support popping up all across the heartland, I did urge him never to take it for granted. He needed to guard that support like his greatest treasure and to remember how often good people like these had been burned by the pikers and fakers—false prophets, I called them—who wound up leading our government only to become self-serving political hacks. He needed to nurture that support and roll it around like a warm stone in his pocket. These people understood that maybe—just maybe—the man of their prayers had finally come. With the support of these Americans, Trump had no reason to play the chameleon skedaddling around trying to be all things to all people.

Donald J. Trump had tapped into the mother lode, and he knew it better than anyone else.

His solutions are not always tidy or perfect, but they are a radical departure from the way things have been done in Washington for a very, very long time. In so many ways, Donald Trump is the nuclear option for our times—and the last best option for making America great again.

★CHAPTER ONE★

President Trump joins children at White House Easter Egg Roll

(Official White House Photo by Shealah Craighead)

FIGHTING THE LEXICON OF LUNACY

When Donald Trump and his elegant wife glided down that glass escalator into a political maelstrom on June 16, 2015, few could have imagined just how radically this rough-hewn real estate mogul would revolutionize everything about modern American politics. Nothing—and I mean nothing—would be altered more shockingly than the very language. I'm speaking of the way people discuss politics. The manner in which people argue in Washington. Even the things that nice people are allowed to argue about in politics would be radically altered—turned upside down and inside out—by Donald Trump.

It happened on a Tuesday afternoon. I was in my bright little office three blocks from the U.S. Capitol. Sun flooded through the wall of windows facing southeast three stories above Pennsylvania Avenue. From my desk, I could keep an eye on everyone coming and going across the street at the Tune Inn bar, a legendary Washington establishment featuring reasonably priced cold beer and a menagerie of cobweb-mottled taxidermy. Stuffed deer, bear, jackrabbits, bull skulls, and even a few long guns.

In other words, the Tune Inn is about the only establishment in this whole Federal City that a normal American would walk into and feel right at home.

This may sound a little weird, but I kept an old rifle scope on the windowsill of my lair and enjoyed watching people come and go along the street. Most fun of all was busting people I knew who were skulking in to the Tune Inn at 10 a.m.—and not for breakfast.

Perhaps my greatest achievement along these lines was once holding my phone camera and scope steady enough to snap photographs of friends quaffing beers outside on the sidewalk and then sending them the picture as they sat there. I never could figure out how to erase the scope's crosshairs from the picture, which freaked them out pretty good.

Once I accidentally stumbled into a buddy's divorce when I texted him inquiring as to why he had just walked into the Tune Inn so early in the morning. The friend did not recognize my number and assumed it was from a private detective hired by his wife to spy on him. He stormed back outside to confront the dick. He was relieved when he finally called the number to learn it was just me. But I was sorry to hear about his pending divorce.

So, on this nice June day, I had just filed my column for Wednesday's edition of the *Washington Times*. It was then that my attention was summoned to the spectacle unfolding on my television. There was Donald Trump—descending behind

Melania, who was wearing a brilliant white dress—announcing that he was running for president. Ordinarily, this would not have been particularly remarkable. Donald Trump had talked about running for president in the past, but he had never fully committed to it.

This time was entirely different. The timing was different, of course, but so was everything else. The mood in America was different. And this Trump campaign was going to be different from anything we had ever seen.

The man was a loud, brash-talking brawler from New York City known for his success in the tawdry world of reality television—not normally the resume of a politician who hopes to appeal to conservative, religious Republicans. And in the past, it had not. Flanked by perfectly coifed American flags, Trump wore a red tie, white shirt, and blue suit. Red, white, and blue. Simple. Clear. Bold. No Al Gore "earth tones" here. Nor would you see Trump campaigning in shirt sleeves like George W. Bush.

Trump looked a million miles from John Kerry's ridiculous barn jacket and Mitt Romney's silly ironed blue jeans. And Melania would never be seen in anything as gauche as Hillary Clinton's mauve pantsuits. And never—never, never, never— would you see Donald Trump sweating through a white dress shirt like Barack Obama.

Trump's bold and solid shirt, suit, and tie were to become his uniform as he courted the American people—as if he were a reality star candidate running a reality star campaign for a reality star presidency. But no costume alone would get Donald Trump into the White House. For the long run ahead, he had to be decisively different. He had to go truly bold. And in many ways, that meant that he simply had to be himself.

The single biggest difference about Donald Trump's announcement speech that day in June 2015 was not the staging. Nor was it his shirt-tie-suit combo. It was the language he used—his very own language and his very own demeanor. Donald Trump understood from day one that he could never win the presidency talking the way politicians talk. And he could never win by "acting presidential."

People came to love his hilarious campaign trail shtick where he stands upright behind the podium and woodenly pretends to "act presidential" as he struts around the stage like a toy soldier, muttering meaningless politically correct bromides. It is a still-hilarious shtick that drives crowds wild. But more important, it demonstrates just how utterly useless it would have been for Donald Trump to run as some kind of normal political candidate.

No, this was a man who was out to crash the gates of Washington. And in order to do that, he had to radically upend the way the game of politics is played. He had to start by changing the language.

Such a change would not be easy. And it certainly would not be popular among politicians firmly ensconced in Washington. The royalty of the American political scene—known variously as "the Establishment" or "the elites" or "swamp creatures"—closely guard the language that is spoken in politics. It is a powerful tool in maintaining their grip on power. And the political press slavishly enforces these rules of language. (If you don't speak the language, you don't play the game.)

These people have spent decades establishing this vocabulary and hounding from politics anyone who veers outside the proscribed lines. They are forever culling the herd of politicians for saying things that are stupid, thoughtless, strange, or outside the acceptable range of political orthodoxy.

The result of this ever-vigilant speech police is a stilted, meaningless political vocabulary that's poll tested and riddled with preposterous euphemisms that provide for an infinite number of acceptable phrases that Democrats and Republicans yell back and forth—never actually winning any arguments and not accomplishing anything tangible for the voters they claim to represent.

Speech codes are nothing new. They have been popular among tyrants, despots, and demagogues since the beginning of human politics. Such a speech code was made famous, of course, by George Orwell's dystopian novel *1984*, published in 1949.

In Orwell's fictional country of Oceana, the establishment "Inner Party" uses the official language of "Newspeak" to control the lower population of workers. The Inner Party uses all manner of media—two-way telescreens to microphones to spies—to enforce the Newspeak speech codes and report back any "thoughtcrimes" committed by the working proles. Another tool used by the Inner Party that is vital for controlling the masses is a regime of never-ending, continuous war. Also used are so-called false flag operations perpetuated by the Inner Party but made to appear as being carried out by some purported enemy of the state who may or may not even exist. The whole notion was popularized and updated by the Hunger Games books and movies.

Does any of this sound familiar?

Despite my considerable skepticism of governments in general and the United States government in particular, I have never been a serious believer in extravagant conspiracy theories. Not to disappoint any dear friends, but I believe Elvis Presley is dead and the moon landing was real. But I sure don't blame anyone for being skeptical about any official government explanations for anything. The heaping lies inside the Warren Report's explanation for the assassination of President Kennedy have probably done as much as anything in the past century to corrode the credibility of the federal government.

Or take the mind-blowingly dishonest and conniving conspiracy by former attorney general Eric Holder's Justice Department to run guns into Mexico and drugs back into America. It is further evidence that conspiracy theories are not always just "theories." Also, it proves that there is no limit to what people in power will do to abuse that power for their selfish purposes.

Yes, indeed, power corrupts. Absolute power corrupts absolutely.

THE LEXICON OF LUNACY

It is chilling to read *1984* today, seven decades after George Orwell published it. His ability to predict how established government authorities would use such "Orwellian" tactics to hold on to power is rivaled only by the ability of America's Founders to ward off the very same abuses in some of their wisest elements of our Constitution.

In America, obviously, political leaders don't enforce a "Newspeak" speech code and they certainly do not codify it. They don't have a name for it at all, because to have a name for it would confirm its very existence. But others—outside the established "Inner Party"—do have terms for it. "Political correctness" is probably the most common description.

I call it the Lexicon of Lunacy.

The list of words, terms, and phrases in the Lexicon of Lunacy runs from the ridiculous to the deadly serious. Take the word "cisgender," for example. I don't actually know what it means but I know that we are supposed to use it when we are all tiptoeing around somebody's severe midlife mental breakdown in which they decide to go under the knife to rearrange the sex organs God gave them.

Come to think of it, this is not at all funny. I feel genuinely sorry for anyone who finds himself, herself, or itself that thoroughly confused and lost in life. The only thing that could be worse would be if politicians decided to take that devastatingly depressing sorrow and weaponize it for political use.

Oh yeah, that has already happened.

So, how about this for an actually funny term from the Lexicon of Lunacy. "Overweight" has become a bad word because we don't want to "fat shame" or "body shame" anyone. Instead we call the person "under tall." Or, maybe "height-challenged." Or "girth-oppressed."

Those are funny. My children use them against me all the time.

Others are not funny at all.

The fuzzy term "pro-choice," for instance, is the accepted euphemism for a political stance that favors killing a healthy, live human fetus that is living and developing in its mother's body. In some cases, the term "pro-choice" can even mean the extermination and dismemberment of a healthy, growing fetus that might even be viable outside the womb. Who on earth hears of such a grisly procedure and thinks of the word "choice"? And, of course, the prefix "pro-"?

Less graphic but devastating in other ways are terms such as "free trade." "Free trade" has become a mantra for hyperglobalization of the economy in ways that punish American workers, wildly enrich Wall Street and the captains of industry, and obliterate the ideals that have always separated America from the rest of the world.

Some of the best euphemisms, lies, and distortions in the Lexicon of Lunacy deal with illegal immigration. To be crystal clear, "illegal immigration" is when illegal aliens illegally enter our country without permission and illegally attempt to illegally reside and illegally work here.

Now, in the Lexicon of Lunacy, this activity is termed "undocumented." And it is the only acceptable word to describe illegal aliens who are living illegally in the United States. Some of these illegal aliens illegally overstayed their visas to be living here illegally. Others illegally crossed the border to be living here illegally. Many of these illegal aliens also work in the United States illegally.

But, in our crazy political world, mentioning the word "illegal" in reference to "undocumented" people is considered hateful and even racist.

The problem with using the word "undocumented" is that not only does the term give the wrong impression, but it is a flat-out lie. "Undocumented" suggests illegal aliens have documentation that proves they are somehow here legally, but they just don't have those documents on them at the moment.

No! If you are an illegal alien, documents proving you are legal do not exist! And if said illegal alien manufactures papers or documents to illegally and dishonestly suggest that he is somehow, in fact, here in the country legally, then he has committed additional crimes.

By browbeating people into using terms like "undocumented" to describe people who are actually "illegal aliens," lawless leftists successfully push their dishonest agenda to erase what it means to be a citizen of the United States of America. It is their way of obliterating the sacred notion of "equal justice under law."

Perhaps my favorite euphemism in the Lexicon of Lunacy deployed by American political establishment royalty is a term that is astonishingly dishonest and mercilessly subversive: "identity politics."

The term, of course, describes a certain political strategy that is highly favored nowadays by Democrat politicians and the hacks they hire to do some of their nastiest dirty work. Republicans also use "identity politics" sometimes, but far less.

What is remarkable about "identity politics" is what an entirely accepted political strategy it has become today, sixty-six years after the Supreme Court declared segregation in public schools unconstitutional. Even the great media titans talk about "identity politics" as if it were just some innocuous strategy for reaching voters.

In fact, it is not just another obnoxious example of political correctness. It is the most insidious betrayal of the civil rights movement in America, in which a color-blind equality was so valiantly fought for. "Identity politics" represents everything that noble leaders like Martin Luther King devoted their lives to fighting against.

"Identity politics" is a strategy that separates black people and white people and Asian people and Hispanic people into different groups, based on their ethnicity and racial "identity." Democrats go even further by dividing men and women and gays and Muslims and Jews and Christians and assigning them all to different camps.

Then Democrats tailor specific messages for each of the

groups, often playing one group off another. It is a vicious mockery of Martin Luther King's plea for all Americans to be judged not by the color of our skin, but by the content of our character. Yet it goes on openly and unapologetically in American politics today.

If public schools were doing it, it would be called "segregation." If a town were doing it, it would be called a throwback to "Jim Crow" laws. If a storekeeper were doing it, it would be called "racial profiling." If a regular person walking down the street were doing it, it would be called exactly what it is: racism. Yet, in the world of Democrat politics, it is considered mainstream political strategy.

Standing on the sidelines, observing all of this dishonest language concealing such deep corruption, listening to all the meaningless pablum from the Potomac swamp basin, was Donald J. Trump. And, like the brilliant salesman and master marketer that he has always been, Trump saw an opportunity to inject a little Hudson River honest, brash talk into the conversation. His amazing instincts clearly told him that voters all over would love it.

When Trump jumped into the presidential race in 2015, he was a well-known figure. He had been in the hot glare of the New York tabloid media for decades. Everything from the unveiling of golden buildings that bore his name to raunchy details about his various divorces made headlines. His business accomplishments in the real estate world and his success as a reality television star put him on par with a tiny handful of stars known around the world by one name.

But when Trump descended the escalator in Trump Tower that day, he had made political headlines more recently for something entirely different.

Four years earlier, Trump shocked the political world by launching a campaign questioning whether President Barack Obama was born in the United States. For the entire political-media establishment inside Washington, D.C., this merely proved that Donald Trump was some kind of crazy conspiracy loon. For these establishment people, it also proved Trump was a racist.

At the time, any kind of criticism of Obama could draw accusations of racism. Criticism with even a faint hint that Obama was from somewhere else or had loyalties elsewhere would be roundly denounced as racist. And anyone questioning Obama's loyalty would be evicted from the political arena.

I know this personally because back in 2008, Obama campaign officials kicked me off the Obama campaign plane for a column I had written. At the time, I was D.C. bureau chief for the *New York Post*. During the Democrat primary, I had maintained a fairly good relationship with the Obama campaign. Obama was new to the political scene and was, therefore, kind of interesting. We gave him a fair shake.

It also helped that he was running against the *New York Post*'s hometown senator (via Arkansas), Hillary Clinton. Man, we gave her hell in that primary! By the time Obama had dispatched Clinton and the general election had rolled around, nobody in Clinton world was talking to me anymore. But I was still in fairly good standing with the Obama campaign. Until, that is, I wrote a column comparing his position on the Iraq War to that of Republican rival John McCain.

It was a perfectly obvious observation that while McCain was willing to do anything to win the war in Iraq, Obama was willing to walk away from that war, even if it meant defeat for America. I doubt there was a single person supporting

Obama who did not believe that to be true. But by spelling it out in a column, I had by their lights raised a question about Obama's loyalty. This got me into big trouble with the Obama campaign. Anything that raised any negative hint about Obama's allegiance was verboten.

As I was standing at the luggage carousel inside the old terminal at Reagan National Airport waiting for bags, my phone rang. It was Bill Burton from the Obama campaign. That whole day, I had been getting earfuls from various Obama campaign operatives who were angry about my column. But Burton is one of the best when it comes to abusive campaign hacks. He did not disappoint.

When I answered, Burton was midstream in a lengthy, expletive-filled tirade about what a despicable reporter I was and what a dishonest rag I worked for. I don't remember everything he said but I remember standing there happily listening as I watched the bags go round and round the luggage carousel.

After explaining that I was kicked off the campaign plane for good, Burton slowed down and told me how Obama had endured some of the most outrageous, disgusting, and racist things written about him in the course of the primary and general election campaign. "But you know, man, that column you wrote is the single most insulting thing that has ever been written about him!" (Quote cleaned up to remove profanity.)

I didn't know what to say except, "Thanks. That's a real compliment."

At that, he hung up on me as my bags finally arrived.

Now, obviously, the notion that there was something racist about observing Obama's position on the Iraq War is patently absurd. But it highlights just how sensitive and dictatorial the campaign was.

After Obama's historic election, the *Washington Post* reported on the campaign's decision to boot me off the plane in a profile of incoming press secretary Robert Gibbs: "In September, Charles Hurt, the *New York Post*'s Washington bureau chief, was barred from the campaign plane after writing in a column that Obama 'simply doesn't care if we win or lose the war in Iraq.'"

Gibbs, according to the profile by Howard Kurtz, called the charge in my column "as irresponsible a line as I've read in this country in years."

It should be said that any reporter covering the Obama campaign certainly witnessed disgusting, clearly racist verbal attacks on Obama. I happen to come from the school of thought that giving such people a megaphone to spew their hateful talk is not the right answer. That small minority of people have already been marginalized by society.

But by lumping all criticism of Obama into—or at least uncomfortably close to—the dirty pile of racist garbage does more than just minimize the seriousness of racism. It becomes a tool to silence all good people who have a fair criticism about the guy.

This dynamic is felt far beyond the Obama campaign plane.

Anywhere in America, well-meaning people who are absolutely not racist have felt the sting of that accusation for merely leveling a fair criticism of President Obama. No matter what your politics are, that is not a healthy political environment. In a free country, no one is beyond criticism, especially if that person is the most powerful person on the planet.

So, sure, Donald Trump earned the undying enmity of the political establishment for cranking up such a loud campaign in 2011 questioning Obama's birth certificate. But outside Washington, Trump simply proved he was willing to talk about things and ask questions about things that the entire political establishment had deemed unmentionable—even racist.

Having already demonstrated his unflinching willingness to go crashing wildly into the choppy waters of political incorrectness, Donald Trump was ready to announce his campaign for the presidency. From the first words, it was clear this would be a different kind of candidate running a different kind of campaign.

"Wow. Whoa," he said, admiring the crowd cheering him from all sides and the balcony above.

"That is some group of people. *Thousands*," he said.

That line still gets me. Literally, within the first ten words of Trump's campaign—even before he actually announced his intentions—Trump was focused on crowd size. Much more on that later. But suffice it to say that in the years since Trump uttered those words, he has talked a great deal about crowd sizes, and it has driven his enemies absolutely out of their minds. Which, in turn, brings wild, lusty cheers from audiences who pack monster truck arenas to see their president perform.

After admiring the assembled crowd, he thanked them. He called it "an honor" to have them in "Trump Tower."

Never. Stop. Selling.

I think it was along about that moment in his speech that I said to myself, This guy could be our next president.

His message was simple. Clear. Pro-American. He was selling something. He was telling a story. After seven years of bitter disappointment and the wasted opportunities of Barack Obama's nerdy, professorial, lecture-some presidency, this guy could be just what America needs, I thought.

Quickly, Trump got back to the size of his crowd.

"This is beyond anybody's expectations," he beamed. "There's been no crowd like this."

Then he attacked. Ferociously.

Some of the Republicans who had already announced for president botched their kickoffs. The air conditioner didn't work, or something. "They sweated like dogs," Trump sneered.

Worse, their crowds were too small for the rooms they hired.

And then the kill shot: "How are they going to beat ISIS?" he asked.

"I don't think it's gonna happen. Our country is in serious trouble."

It's a fair point. If you cannot pull off a simple announcement speech on television, then how on earth can you possibly be expected to destroy the most diabolical and determined jihad of our time?

There is a larger point here as well. It has to do with language.

In the very first moments of his announcement speech, Donald Trump was declaring a pact with American voters. Earlier, he had proved his willingness to go wildly off script from establishment officialdom when he brazenly questioned Obama's birth certificate.

Now he was promising to use the same scalding rhetoric and blunt honesty to expose and fix a whole host of grievous maladies facing regular Americans across the country.

Maladies that had crept into American society over the decades under the blind—or, often, encouraging—eye of political leaders in both parties.

Terrorism, globalism, "free" trade, illegal immigration, *legal* immigration. Trump was willing to be as belligerent as he needed to be in order to finally stand up to ISIS, China, Japan, Mexico, and the entire global world order.

Trump shrewdly understood in that moment that if political candidates were incapable of speaking bluntly about thorny issues, or if they shied away from harshly identifying America's enemies, then there would be no hope for anything ever getting better.

Standing there in my office, watching this amazing spectacle unfold, it was that different way of talking that most gripped my attention. A wildly fresh vocabulary with sharp notes of brazenly impolitic honesty.

"The U.S. has become a dumping ground for everybody else's problem," Trump said, just a few lines into the speech.

My goodness, I thought. Nobody in Washington talks like this. But it sounds like exactly what you hear just about anywhere if you leave Washington, D.C., or New York City.

"When Mexico sends its people, they're not sending their best. They're not sending you. They're not sending *you*," he said, karate chopping the air.

"They're sending people that have lots of problems and they're bringing those problems to us. They're bringing drugs, they're bringing crime, they're rapists, and some, I assume, are good people."

On its face, this statement is technically true. Illegals from Mexico (and other places south of the border) come into the United States. They smuggle drugs into the country. They certainly commit crimes (including illegally crossing our border). And some of them are indeed rapists.

Trump was highlighting a real, destructive and expensive problem that a lot of American voters care deeply about. Yet almost nobody in Washington cares about fixing it.

Democrats are desperate to change the voting electorate. So, they want every warm body they can get into the country to hustle to the voting booth. Republicans, being more business friendly, are delighted to turn a blind eye on a process that floods our country with cheap labor.

The only group without a voice in this debate were millions of regular American voters. Until Trump announced his campaign.

Donald Trump's furious assault on the political establishment brought condemnations from every corner of it. Sure, those people were perfectly content letting political sleeping dogs lie. China ripping off America was no big deal for them. Free trade was going gangbusters for the stock market and Wall Street. Everybody who was anybody was making a killing off illegal immigration. Cheap nannies for all!

But the seething rebukes of Trump and his announcement speech were about so much more than just those issues. They were about Trump's language, his rough-and-tumble demeanor, and his willingness to court such political upheaval.

In her memoir, former first lady Michelle Obama eviscerated the man who followed her husband into the White House for just this. Trump's questioning of Obama's birth certificate, she wrote, "was crazy and mean-spirited, of course, its underlying bigotry and xenophobia hardly concealed."

Again, any hint of questioning Obama's American loyalty was deemed racist. Such a questioner was not just called out as dishonest or stupid or uninformed. They were flat-out racist for questioning Obama's alliances.

That was not all Michele Obama had to say about Trump and his style of politics. Trump's birth certificate inquiry "was also dangerous, deliberately meant to stir up the wingnuts and kooks," she wrote. "What if someone with an unstable mind loaded a gun and drove to Washington? What if that person went looking for our girls? Donald Trump, with his loud and reckless innuendos, was putting my family's safety at risk. And for this I'd never forgive him."

Wow. Perhaps Michelle Obama spoke too soon when she said that she was finally proud of her country once her husband got elected.

But I have to ask: What is more incendiary? Asking questions about where a political opponent was born? Or accusing a political opponent of deliberately and willfully trying to inspire "wingnuts and kooks" to assassinate the daughters of a president?

While we're at it, what about a president who wades into local police issues around the country and his only contribution is to inject race into them? What about a president who goes around the world apologizing for America and giving long lectures about how America is exceptional, you know, like every other country on the planet is exceptional in its own way. In other words, nothing exceptional whatsoever about America. What about a president who belittles Americans for their "guns" and their "religion"?

After eight years of insufferable academia out of the White House, it should have been little surprise that American voters would be in the mood for something very different. They would be looking for a guy who speaks bluntly and paints vivid pictures. A guy who spent years savoring his time talking to the workers and tradesmen who built his buildings, and learned to talk like them. Above all, he was listening and listening and taking to heart what he was hearing.

Every now and then, some reporter churns a Trump speech through some word program on the Internet that calculates the grade level the speech was written at. As in sixth-grade level, meaning a sixth grader could understand it. And these simpering, obnoxious, arrogant asses somehow think that speaking so plainly is an insult, when Trump—along with American voters—knows it is actually the highest, most honest achievement there is.

INDEPENDENT AUTHENTICITY VOTER

Strangely, this was a counterintuitive gambit for some of the very same voters who wound up stunning the political establishment by voting for Trump—after having voted for Barack Obama. Twice! I call them the independent authenticity voters. They don't much care about parties and don't particularly like Washington politics. But every four years they generally turn out and vote. And when the noise of the campaign gets as loud as it does every four years, they are reminded of how much they despise politics and most politicians. But they mostly turn out and vote.

Overwhelmingly, they choose the lesser bastard. The least dishonest one. The one they think comes closest to being genuine and authentic. In 2008, that was obviously Barack Obama. His hopeful campaign about neither red America nor blue America but one red, white, and blue America resonated with these voters. Funnily enough, the late senator John McCain would have appealed to these very voters eight years earlier when he was still a true political "maverick" and before he got co-opted by Democrats and the media (I repeat myself) to kneecap Republicans at every turn. As bad as things were in 2012, President Obama still had enough authenticity left in the tank to beat the hopelessly repackaged Mitt Romney.

These voters yearned for someone authentic to be president. Most horrifying to mainstream political observers is the number of voters who voted for President Barack Obama—twice!—because they thought he was that authentic nonpolitician. Oh, how they were betrayed!

The accepted language of politics is defended by those who practice it as merely polite and responsible. And this is often true. I know many decent politicians and staffers and journalists who embrace polite language. And they are disgusted by anything else in the political arena.

If the 2016 election proved anything, it proved that Donald Trump was exactly right. There was, after all, a tremendous thirst out there for something different. Something new. Above all, something authentic.

So, from the very first lines of his announcement speech that day at the foot of his glass escalator, Mr. Trump proved to be impolitic. Unpolished. Dripping with authenticity. That guy you know who talks rough, who doesn't own a set of church clothes but would be the first person you would call if you found yourself in a life-threatening situation and needed some really dirty work handled.

Trump knew at that moment that he had to break through all the soft, white noise of modern American politics. All the fake niceties of acceptable political speech. After all, it was a lie and had been for a very long time. Behind all those fake niceties were the raw, brutal realities of vicious politics played by the nastiest of operatives going back decades. They peddled in the most dishonest, soul-crushing, character-destroying sewage that you could imagine—but then wore nice seersucker suits at garden parties, talking all sorts of high-minded pleasantries.

Yuck!

Donald Trump saw all of this for exactly what it was. It was a fraud. Whether it was trade, immigration, wars, spending, or taxes—it was all a fraud. The American people were getting taken to the cleaner's financially, and the American people were getting sold out as losers.

And Trump wasn't even president yet! He was still just one of sixteen people vying for the Republican nomination. If you polled the media that day, every single reporter in all of politics would have given Trump a zero percent chance of winning the nomination, let alone the presidency.

After the speech was over, I called my office at the *Washington Times* and told my editor to scrap the column I had filed—that a new one was on the way. I endorsed Donald Trump, something I had never done before in a newspaper column. Because, after all, who gives a crap what I think about anything? But this was clearly something different. The speech was brilliant. It was daring, to be sure, but it also reflected an enormous amount of intentional thought. Trump had been listening very closely to voters. He had also been talking to some very smart people who clearly follow politics closely and understood the political landscape far better than any of the self-anointed geniuses inside the Beltway.

So I picked up the phone and called Steve Bannon, a friend who I knew liked to dabble in the more contrarian world of counterpolitics. We agreed the speech was great and, of course, Bannon told me he had been talking to Trump. A speech had been written. Bannon had seen it as late as the night before, he said. But the speech Trump delivered on live television to the country was entirely different than the one that had been prepared.

"Yeah, he didn't read the speech," Bannon marveled. "He got up there and just decided to wing it!"

Even at that point, Trump was not to be handled or scripted or managed or staffed. He was going on nothing but his own raw political instincts. And in the end, voters trusted Donald J. Trump to remain in character more than they trusted any politician to keep his campaign promises.

That turned out to be a pretty smart bet.

★CHAPTER TWO★

President Trump looks on as First Lady Melania Trump addresses military personnel and their families on September 15, 2017.

(Official White House Photo by Shealah Craighead)

STORMING
THE GATES

D uring Donald Trump's short career as an official politician, his most appealing qualification may have been that he was not one of the lifetime pols who've been lying around Washington for decades, eating fancy food and spinning out miles of federal regulations, racking up oceans of national debt, and entangling us in costly, devastating foreign wars with no strategic agenda and no end in sight.

Clearly, Trump has used his outsider status to masterfully storm the gates of Washington and topple Republican Party leadership. But there is so much more for him to do. Draining the sleaze-ridden swamp of its hydra-headed monsters is an even greater challenge.

Consider the lobby industry that prides itself on influencing and controlling important legislation as it moves through Congress. That control is based on the tentacles of money-laden special interests that celebrate their grip on the national government by laying out the big bucks wherever needed to keep the wheels spinning, to keep the right people in the right places. In doing so, these unelected powerhouses create an ever-greater divide between the government and the citizens it is supposed to serve.

The lobby industry attracts some of the most morally bankrupt politicians from both the House and the Senate. These former members of Congress, having sated themselves at the public trough, now sit like bloated toads on the swamp's lily pads, flicking their tongues out for the sweetest of delicacies. Having sold their souls and cashed in whatever credibility they possessed, they ply the corridors of Congress, schmoozing former colleagues and staffers to influence legislation that governs the lives of millions of Americans.

And then we have the career "public servants" who work in high staff positions in Congress and stay just long enough to make their career move to K Street, where they can make the big bucks serving whatever masters give them the most money to use their skills and influence in any given area.

So, if you want a treasure chest of easy money and big steaks, Washington is the place for you. It is America's insulated cocoon of opulence where the pay scale is high and the housing prices are stable—all at the expense of the ordinary people across the land who are paying the bills and suffering the idiocy that pours from the place. And no idiocy is greater than the brutal national debt of more than $20,000,000,000,000 that these irresponsible bureaucrats have charged against the futures of our generations to come.

All of this is a formula for disaster that, finally, Americans seem to be waking up to. That, of course, is a chief reason why so many see Donald Trump as their only hope.

But even with so much wrong in Washington that should have been fixed decades ago, Trump brings to his job considerable political savvy of his own. His gut political instincts are the very best of any politician I have ever been around.

"People like to say I am new to politics," he told me once. "In a lot of ways, I have been in politics all my life. I was like the mayor—*the king!*—of City Hall in New York City! Can you imagine how much time I had to spend down there to get my buildings built?"

Part of Trump's political genius is his ability to scare the hell out of everyone in the room. He says things that are plainly true—but things nobody in a position of authority is willing to say. He lists objectives everyone agrees should be the goal—yet nobody says them because no one believes they can actually be achieved, or those in power pay lip service to them with no intention of doing anything about them.

A strong and simple example of this is Trump's decision to move the U.S. embassy in Israel from Tel Aviv to that nation's capital at Jerusalem. Not that it was unusual for Trump to make that promise while a candidate for president. Presidents of both parties going back at least to Bill Clinton had made the same promise as candidates.

The only shocker is that Donald Trump actually meant it. And made good on it. It didn't matter to him that it might offend some people in the Middle East, where they have frittered away decades hopelessly negotiating peace. Or offend others in the Middle East who have been cynically harpooning peace there for decades. In fact, maybe offending some people might do the trick. At least it would be trying something different from all the failed efforts of the past. Most of all, he believed it was the right thing to do so, he did it—a refreshingly different way to govern.

Certainly, Donald Trump's insistence on approaching every problem anew can be mightily frustrating for supporters—a little like he is trying to reinvent the wheel every day. Some cringe when President Trump asks in his little-boy wonderment, why in the world do we have all of these nuclear weapons if we don't intend to use them? Actually, that is a profoundly intelligent question and the answer is terrifyingly simple. We should not have all those weapons unless the world reasonably believes we really will use them.

Others freak out when President Trump wonders aloud why we don't have huge military parades down Pennsylvania Avenue. For many of us, however, it is an interesting question.

Even some of Trump's rare early supporters in Washington sometimes chafe under Trump's refusal to play any of the routine campaign games or abide by any of the Washington political niceties. They need to keep in mind that he has never played by anybody else's notions of protocol, and it is not surprising that he doesn't respect the process and norms of regular political campaigns.

Truth is, he probably could not have done so if he tried. As all of Washington became obsessed with the silly canard about "collusion" between the Trump campaign and Russia, some of us would joke that the Trump campaign could not even manage to collude with itself. So, it was hilarious to imagine the campaign trying to collude with a giant foreign power that also happened to be an arch global enemy.

One experienced political operative, an observer who realized Donald Trump's potential from the very beginning, became frustrated over how poorly the campaign communicated with people like herself who wanted to help. In Washington, these people are called "surrogates" and they go on television—often armed with information provided by campaigns—to make the best arguments on behalf of the candidate. Everybody does it and it all kind of equals out so that you have a type of proxy war going on over the airwaves among various spokespeople.

With a mixture of despair and amusement, my friend who wanted to help Trump was delighted when the campaign finally began sending people like her "talking points." But when she read them, she was astonished. Never had she worked for any campaign that seemed to insist on doing everything—from the tiniest of little things to the biggest of big things—completely differently.

No matter what the issue at hand—Donald Trump's position on taxes or immigration to the latest scandalous accusation—the Trump campaign's "talking points" always began the same way.

First: "Donald Trump is a builder. He builds buildings."

And then the "talking points" would go on to talk about the need to lower taxes or clamp down on illegal immigration.

To people in Washington and in politics generally, this was gibberish in a foreign language. But I maintain that it is exactly that kind of mentality directly from the candidate himself that got Trump elected. He was not just some glib and gifted speaker who had been a community organizer or a personal injury lawyer or a lifelong political hack. He was a business guy who builds buildings. And if you didn't believe him, you could go to New York City or Las Vegas or Chicago and see it for yourself.

And no matter what President Obama might say, Trump *did* build those buildings.

It wasn't just the little things that set Donald Trump and his presidential campaign apart from everybody else. It was the big things, too. Early on, friends of mine around Washington with whom I had always agreed on politics were aghast at Donald Trump. I can hear my friends railing now: "The man cannot be trusted! He says whatever he needs to say! He will destroy the Constitution!"

In all honesty, I did sometimes worry about where Trump would be on the Constitution. That is a pretty big deal to me. Watching Barack Obama nonchalantly shred the Constitution on a routine basis is a big reason why in 2015 I was willing to take a flier with the most outrageous, disruptive, and unpredictable candidate in my lifetime.

But I never bought that whole trope about how Donald Trump would trash the Constitution. After all, any guy who has been in as many lawsuits as Trump must surely cherish having a set of rules by which everyone must play. Otherwise, you never win in court and you never get what you want.

With President Trump, that has proven true.

———————

From the very start of the Trump campaign, when veteran political reporters I had known for years seemed to be having nervous breakdowns in public nearly every day about something Donald Trump had done, I kept thinking about all the things President Obama had done. And all of his predecessors.

Combined, they had piled up more than $20 trillion in real debt upon our children, grandchildren, and great-grandchildren. They could never reasonably be expected to pay it off in their lifetimes. That debt is even more unimaginably massive when you tally up all the unfunded obligations that the government owes people over the coming decades.

Meanwhile, the U.S. government has never been more gargantuan. It has become so powerful that it reaches into nearly every crevice of American life today. A farmer is prohibited from drawing water from a pond on his own land so that his own hogs might drink—without the probing approval of the federal government. A baker in Lakewood, Colorado, cannot operate a bakery without the federal government intruding. A peaceful farmer cannot sell fresh milk produced by his own cows without risking a federal SWAT team from the United States Department of Agriculture launching a predawn raid with armed commandos rounding up his sleeping family in their pajamas.

Yet, never has this same all-powerful federal government been less answerable to the American people. Legislators from both parties have gradually and gladly handed over more and more authority to the president in the White House—so long as that president is of the same party. But no matter which party the president might be in, he never surrenders back that authority when he leaves office.

The result is that the branch of government closest to the people—Congress generally and the House of Representatives specifically—has ceded more and more authority to the executive branch. Gone are the days when committee chairmen in Congress were celebrated for grinding the entire federal government to a halt in order to protect some constituent back home from the tyrannical hand of the federal government.

No matter Donald Trump's imperfections, he was at least willing to question all the "wisdom" that has dominated the media complex for decades in Washington and led to this terrible state of affairs. He was at least willing to ask the uncomfortable questions. And, best of all, he was willing to listen carefully to the only people who matter: the voters.

Throughout the campaign, the Great White Media churned out silly story after silly story about an endless string of nonscandals. All of it was designed to make Donald Trump look unfit for the White House. "Unpresidential," as they all liked to say.

Wisely, Trump embraced the moniker and pretty much vowed to serve as "unpresidentially" as possible. If "presidential" is what has gotten us into this mess over so many years, then let's try "unpresidential" for a change. Obviously, detractors want to equate "unpresidential" with "unqualified" or "dangerous." For them, I always thought a great Trump campaign bumper sticker would have been simply, "Vote Trump. You Can't Screw It Up."

It's similar, in fact, to his message to black voters who have been taken advantage of, disrespected, and disregarded by the Democrat Party for more than a half century now: "What have you got to lose?"

One of the most obvious ways President Trump stands out from the rest of Washington politicians is his exhaustive use of Twitter. For enthusiastic supporters, our only concern is that he does not send enough messages over Twitter. For others, even many who work for him faithfully, they wish he would knock it off. It allows him to get drawn into unnecessary controversies that his campaign staff—and now his White House staff—has to handle.

This, of course, begs the larger question of what on earth campaign and administration staffers are supposed to spend their time doing other than helping explain and carry out the vision of the candidate or president they are working for. Perhaps the best example of President Trump's adventurism over Twitter were his claims about the size of the crowd that attended his inauguration in January 2017.

He was pilloried by partisan detractors as well as almost everybody in the so-called mainstream media. They portrayed him as some kind of insecure, childish liar obsessed with unimportant things.

Well, let's consider that a little more closely. For example, is crowd size unimportant? Obviously, looking back, the size of the crowds showing up for Donald Trump's campaign rallies clearly predicted that he had tapped into something hugely popular and might win not only the Republican nomination, but the general election as well. Perhaps if all the experts in the media had spent a little more time paying attention to the enormous enthusiasm of those massive crowds showing up at Trump campaign rallies, they might not have been quite so shellacked with surprise on the night of the election.

Anyway, if crowd size is so unimportant, then why have CNN and the *Washington Post* and the *New York Times* spilled so many barrels of ink and electrified so many terabytes of words on the Internet desperately trying to knock down President Trump's claims about the size of the crowd at his inauguration? Why would any organization supposedly dedicated to gathering the news spend so much time focusing on something that they themselves claim is so entirely irrelevant?

I actually do not believe President Trump's focus on crowd size is unimportant. Nor do I believe it reveals some dangerous streak of childish narcissism. What everybody in the media and in our broken political system fails to understand is that President Trump's focus on things like crowd size actually reveals something very positive and productive: He is a businessman who just might have, at some point, sported a sign in his office like this: "If You Can't Measure It, You Can't Manage It."

The reason President Trump "obsesses" over things like crowd size is that it is a simple, measurable metric. It is a way for him to evaluate how well he is doing something, as compared to other people who are trying to do the same thing. It is why he wants the biggest plane and the best helicopter and the tallest building that offers the best taco bowls. It is why he cares about how many people follow him on Twitter.

You see, in Washington, everybody survives without anybody ever missing a lunch because there is no measurable metric by which people are objectively judged. It is all BS and "messaging" and posturing. Becoming a chief of staff for a member of Congress, for example, is like becoming a "made man" in the mafia. As a friend of mine says, you will never miss a lunch in this town again if you become a "made man" in either political party.

And so the beat goes on and everybody wrings their hands and complains about Donald Trump and his insistence on using Twitter to get out the messages that the media refuses to report. How humiliating it must be for the grand poohbahs of the media to be bypassed each and every day by a president unwilling to have his words and actions distorted by the irresponsible media.

One of President Trump's most successful cabinet secretaries told me about how often people ask him what President Trump is really like in person, behind closed doors. The secretary laughed and said he always answers the same way.

"Are you on the Internet?" the cabinet secretary asks. "Ever heard of Twitter? Well, if you go on the Internet and find Twitter and look for President Trump's tweets, read those and you'll know exactly what President Trump is like in person, behind closed doors."

This is, of course, completely true.

———————

A solid two years into Trump's presidency, Americans were treated to one of the most ridiculous stories ever produced about a sitting president. President Trump, some cutting-edge Internet sleuths reported, was spending an inordinate amount of his day in "executive time." Too much time, anyway, as determined by these Internet sleuths.

This story broke like it was Watergate.

"President Donald Trump had about three times as much free time planned for last Tuesday as work time, according to his private schedule," reported one team of reporters, breathlessly heralding that they had somehow gotten ahold of the president's personal schedule.

"The president was slated for more than nine hours of 'Executive Time,' a euphemism for the unstructured time Trump spends tweeting, phoning friends, and watching television," this team of reporters wrote on the Internet. "Official meetings, policy briefings, and public appearances— typically the daily work of being president—consumed barely more than three hours of his day."

The most amazing part of this "story" to me was that two years into Trump's presidency and more than three years after he had launched his presidential campaign, there were still reporters in Washington who were somehow surprised that this is a president who operates differently from other presidents. He has different work habits. He approaches things differently.

Duh.

One of the most ignorant, ill-informed, and misguided attacks on President Trump is that he is some kind of bullheaded autocrat who surrounds himself with yes-men and yes-women to whom he does not listen.

Anyone who has ever spent time around Trump can tell you what an absurd mischaracterization this is. It is certainly true that President Trump is capable of calling up people and launching into *Heart of Darkness* tirades about his political enemies or how dishonest the media is in covering him. Anybody who has ever watched President Trump at a campaign rally should already know that.

But more often than not, those personal phone calls to people involve him calling up to ask an endless array of questions about everything under the sun.

Riding home late one night with my brother after spending a week in Washington, I got an email from the White House. President Trump wanted to talk. I called and got patched through.

For thirty minutes as my brother drove us through the moonless dark of the foothills of rural Virginia from Nelson County to Pittsylvania County, President Trump peppered me with questions about the policy fights of the day, whether he was winning the political arguments and what voters were paying attention to.

Now, I would be the first to offer that President Trump has plenty smarter people than me to be talking to. Heck, his own gut political instincts are the best I have ever seen. But those political instincts are not by accident. He feeds and informs those instincts by being a voracious consumer of information from people he talks to.

"He doesn't listen" is by far the most dishonest critique leveled against Donald Trump. How else do you think he enters politics with a campaign and a message more perfectly tailored to the Republican electorate than anything offered by the two dozen seasoned Republican politicians in the race?

He succeeded by being the most careful and calculating listener of anyone else in the field. At the same time, he nurtured the true confidence to make his own decisions and then remain faithful to that remarkable internal gyroscope that feeds and balances his political instincts.

———————————

I was covering Congress back before the whole Tea Party revolt pulverized the Republican Party. Establishment legislators in Washington still had a pretty firm grip on the Grand Old Party. But it was obvious that trouble was brewing. Republicans had enjoyed an historic "revolution" in the previous decade, winning control of the House and the Senate. George W. Bush had won the 2000 election and would go on to win reelection. Yet the federal government and the tentacles reaching deep into every facet of American life did not appear to be receding.

Whenever I interviewed a self-professed conservative Republican, I asked them all the same stock question. If the Republican Party gained enough control of Washington and you could eliminate three departments of the federal government in an instant, what would those be?

The response was as astonishing as it was dispiriting. Nearly every Republican I ever asked this just stared back, blinking. It was a question that had never occurred to them. It had never dawned on them that voters just might be serious about wanting to slash the federal bureaucracy.

After just a few years in Washington, I had compiled my own list of departments and duties of the federal government I would abolish if anybody gave me the chance.

Department of Labor? Gone. Education Department? Eliminated, with malice. U.S. Junk Mail Service? Gone.

U.S. Department of Transportation? Let the states deal with it. Defense Department? Keep that one but return to its original name: War Department.

Office of Management and Budget? I actually would not eliminate that one. I would suspend the department, fire every employee, and suspend the current OMB director until such time as they figured out how to balance the federal budget. I am sorry, but there are not even criminal enterprises that manage to continue operations after having racked up $22 trillion in debt.

Needless to say, when I interviewed self-described "conservative" Republicans in Congress and they could not even list three major parts of the federal government they would like to see eliminated, I was shocked. Clearly, this meant that the dreams of so many regular conservative voters that one day the federal Leviathan might get tamed were entirely unrealistic. Perhaps even more alarming, voters were electing Republicans under the clearly false impression that they were actually serious about the concept of limited government.

By the time Donald Trump got rolling in his campaign during the summer of 2015, I had these wonderful recurring fantasies. Everybody was so aghast that a reality TV star was making such a big splash. This was a guy who called employees into his conference room before the TV cameras and asked them rapid-fire questions, grilling them in the harshest fashion possible. And then, more often than not, he would jab a finger at them and declare: "You're fired!"

While hundreds in the media and politics were freaking out, I was chuckling and praying for the day Trump would get into the White House, call every single one of his cabinet secretaries into the office and, right in front of the TV cameras rolling live, give each one seven minutes to defend the vital purpose of their department. After seven minutes, the failed secretaries would stand before the Resolute Desk and see President Donald Trump jab his finger their way and say, "You're fired!" Their entire departments would be eliminated right there, live on national television. Audiences would love it! The ratings would be higher than *The Apprentice* and all the *Survivor*s combined!

The lucky few cabinet secretaries who made the cut and survived would be called back to the Oval Office in the following weeks. Live, on national television, each would be given a stark ultimatum: cut 25 percent out of your department. Each would have one week. Or President Trump would do it for them, perhaps even allowing the American people to vote from home on how best to eliminate 25 percent out of the budget of each remaining cabinet department.

After all, American voters back home have a whole lot more experience budgeting within their means than anybody in Washington.

Now, obviously, these daydreams on my part were a bit fantastical. There was a pretty good chance that President Trump would not, in fact, turn the federal government into an *Apprentice/Survivor* game show on national television. And, in fact, he has not done that.

But, still, there was a solid 10 percent chance that he *might* do it. At the very least, it would have been the "worst-case scenario" in the minds of all the Never Trumpers freaking out about his candidacy. And still, it was a better idea than what any of them had ever come up with to tame the federal government. In any event, there might have been only a 10 percent chance that Donald Trump would launch such a circus of firing, but there was a negative percent chance that Jeb Bush or any of the rest of the so-called conservatives running for president would.

In the early 2000s, long before voters sicced Donald Trump on Washington, Republicans were doing swimmingly well, at least in terms of political power inside the Beltway. They held the White House and both chambers of Congress. So, what did Republicans have to show for their years of conservative reign? I am sure there are some victories they could point to. Chief among them would be the tax cuts. But otherwise the big picture was pretty bleak. Especially in terms of fiscal issues.

During Republican control of the House of Representatives between 1994 and 2006, federal debt nearly doubled to $8.5 trillion, from $4.7 trillion. By the time President Bush left office in 2008, that debt had jumped to over $10 trillion.

In terms of policy, conservatives had little to crow about. One of the very first initiatives President Bush embraced after winning the White House in 2000 was to extend an olive branch to Senator Ted Kennedy. Together they hatched a huge new federal program that gave federal bureaucrats all sorts of new ways to meddle with public education around the country: it was called "No Child Left Behind." It was a running joke back then about which children of these vaunted political dynasties was kept from being left behind by this bill. Was it the Bushes or the Kennedys?

Either way, the program proved to be as big a bipartisan disaster as it was a bipartisan "success" when they passed it. By 2015, the whole thing was scrapped and its duties turned over to state educators.

The other big "success" of that period came in 2003, just in time for President Bush to get reelected. To be fair, he had pushed valiantly for privatizing Social Security. At the very least it would keep the kleptocrats in Congress from raiding the retirement accounts of innocent American taxpayers.

Democrats, dishonest as ever, slimed it as some kind of sop to Wall Street. I had a standard question of Democrat lawmakers back then as well. Since they were so opposed to regular Americans getting to privatize their government-mandated retirement program, I wondered, how many of them planned on retiring without a private retirement program of their own?

Needless to say, I never found a single Democrat who intended to rely entirely on Social Security in their golden years. Because, of course, they knew exactly what kind of Ponzi scheme they had turned the program into.

Republicans had better success, however, with their signature achievement that year known as Medicare Part D, a program for paying for medication for seniors. It has long been an initiative pushed by Democrats.

Popular as it may be to give away free medicine, the federal government has an atrocious record of running such entitlement programs efficiently or even honestly. By 2008, this new program—piled on top of entitlement programs already headed for insolvency—was costing tax payers nearly $50 billion annually. It was the single largest expansion of any entitlement program up to that date. (This was before Obamacare and the socialist takeover of the Democrat Party.)

At the time they passed the Democrat proposal, Republicans on Capitol Hill vacillated between saying they had to pass it if they wanted to get reelected in 2004 and lamely promising that the program would save lots of money in the long run. Either way, there was hardly anything "conservative" about it. Little wonder, really, that the Tea Party revolution that hit a few short years later would devour the Republican Party from the inside.

The record of Republican control in Washington—the so-called conservative party—was enough by itself to justify why Republican voters were so eager to run into the arms of Donald Trump. Voters had paid their dues, fallen in line, and held their noses long enough. It was time for a fresh new style and an honest path forward.

Truth is, Donald Trump has set ambitious goals and has significant accomplishments to show for it. But you cannot dispute the fact that he is still up against an increasingly socialist Democrat Party dead set to destroy him at every turn. And he is up against lingering forces of a Republican establishment in Washington that is also eager to destroy him at every turn.

Take the repeal and replacement of Obamacare, a promise Republicans in Washington had been making for years—long before Donald Trump ever announced for president. When he got elected president, he was ready and willing to sign anything Republicans in Congress sent him that repealed and replaced Obamacare. They choked. Or, as President Trump once memorably tweeted: they "chocked."

That had absolutely nothing to do with Donald Trump, except perhaps to underscore how he beat every other Republican for the nomination. Republicans in Washington had been lying to voters, playing empty politics and lazily refusing to do the hard work of actually backing up their promises. And then when Donald Trump got elected—something that establishment Republicans in Washington did not think could happen—they got caught flat-footed on their single biggest promise of the previous two elections.

Despite President Trump's weak partners in Washington Republicans, he has racked up a significant record of success. Much of that has been accomplishments entirely on his own.

For example, moving our embassy in Israel to Jerusalem was no small feat. Nor was it something that particularly improves the everyday lives of regular Americans. The real importance of that move was more symbolic. It was proof to the world that President Trump was willing to do something all of his predecessors were afraid to do. It was proof he really did believe all the things he said during his campaign and he really did intend to make good on those promises. As shocking as that notion is among Washington politicians, it was a welcome relief for actual voters.

Similarly, Trump's withdrawal from the bogus nuclear deal with Iran was not something that affected most Americans in their everyday lives. But it sent a powerful message about his willingness to tread where others feared to go. It also sent shock waves through foreign capitals that President Trump was no longer going to go along with the rest of the world to appease the wishes of the global elite. He intended to usher in a new era of putting America's interest ahead of all others.

That is not to say President Trump intended to foist America on foreign countries. He was not envisioning "regime change" or "nation building" in foreign rat holes like Iraq or Syria. No, while he gladly embraces an "America first" agenda around the world, President Trump has no interest in wasting the money in some fantasy effort to make the whole rest of the world just like us.

So, he did not bomb or invade North Korea, which has developed into a terrifying threat to not only the Korean Peninsula and its immediate neighborhood, but now the entire world. Most of North Korea's "progress" has come during the past two administrations—since North Korea was declared part of the global "Axis of Evil." Instead, President Trump has sought the most robust and high-profile denuclearization talks in history.

Pie in the sky? Perhaps. Naive? Not nearly as naive as thinking you can effect "regime change" and "nation building" around the world without spending massive amounts of money and losing a tragic number of great Americans in the process. And it sure beats the hell out of some nonpeace deal under Obama that gave Iran billions of dollars—hundreds of millions in pallets of cash—in exchange for allowing Iran to keep their nuclear program.

If any doubts remained about President Trump's willingness to rip up global accords and put America first, they vanished when he pulled the United States out of the Paris agreement aimed at combatting global warming.

As with all of these globalist climate-change boondoggles, they are designed to punish the most productive countries on the planet. They are the most devastating to developed countries like the United States that are not only productive but also believe in laws and abiding by agreed-upon rules. It was little wonder that President Obama entered into the agreement in the final months of his administration. He would be long gone by the time the punishing effects of the agreement took a full bite into the American economy and the quality of life of average Americans.

The greatest assault on private property during the Obama administration was the arbitrary rule set by the Environmental Protection Agency that made it possible for federal bureaucrats, with the flick of a pen, to pretty much place land anywhere under the jurisdiction of federal regulators.

Called the Waters of the United States (WOTUS), the 2015 land grab determined that the EPA had control over any backyard ditch, drainage area, or ravine where water gathered during rains. It took control of that property away from landowners and farmers and gave it to federal bureaucrats.

Never in modern times has the federal government— by fiat—attempted a more brazen or widespread invasion of property rights. It was the sort of thing you would see during the Cuban Revolution or under Nicolas Maduro in Venezuela.

The EPA ruling got hung up in court, which is often little solace to innocent landowners. Once the case got diverted to the federal courts, President Trump's EPA dropped the whole matter by reversing the kleptocratic regulation.

President Trump's greatest triumph over the federal bureaucracy was not overturning the EPA's WOTUS land grab. The greatest triumph was clearing the way for Alaska to finally allow drilling for oil underneath the Arctic Ocean. For decades now, so-called environmentalists—the vast majority of whom have never been to Alaska—had successfully blocked efforts to drill for oil in the Arctic National Wildlife Refuge. This despite extensive scientific and industry advancements that allowed such drilling to be done safely and cleanly.

The late Ted Stevens spent forty-one years in the United States Senate and four years before that in the House of Representatives fighting for the right of Alaskans to tap into this vital natural resource. For years, Stevens would fight the environmental lobby on the Senate floor wearing his Incredible Hulk tie, a symbol for how angry he and his fellow Alaskans were to get pushed around by a bunch of environmental lobbyists who had never even set foot in Alaska.

Year after year, decade after decade, Ted Stevens was thwarted. Once, in 2005, it looked like Stevens might finally make good on his promise to open drilling in ANWR, only to be thwarted yet again at the last minute.

"'This has been the saddest day of my life,' said Mr. Stevens, 82, as he watched victory slip away again in his 25-year crusade for drilling in the refuge," reported the *New York Times* at the time.

As improbable as it seems, it would be another eleven years before a Republican would come along and manage to open ANWR to drilling in Alaska. President Trump included a provision to allow drilling in the Republican's 2017 tax overhaul. At first, President Trump was not even aware what a big deal it was until a friend of his in the energy business called him up and told him what a huge victory that would be.

"Are you kidding? That's the biggest thing all by itself!" the friend told Trump, probably during "executive time" in the Oval Office. "Every president since Ronald Reagan has tried to get drilling in ANWR approved."

Buoyed by this, President Trump called his negotiators and told them that whatever they did on the tax overhaul, don't give up drilling in the Arctic National Wildlife Refuge. Sadly, former Alaska senator Ted Stevens had died seven years before in a plane crash and never got to see his dream come true.

★CHAPTER THREE★

President Trump announces his groundbreaking 5G internet plan from the White House (Official White House Photo by Tia Dufour)

THE LEAST RACIST
PERSON IN AMERICA

W hen the Obama campaign kicked me off their plane for writing what the spokesman called "the most insulting" column ever about Barack Obama, I was the Washington Bureau Chief for the *New York Post*. To this day, I would argue that our newspaper was giving a fair shake to Obama and his acolytes. Their dramatic reaction to this particular column was far more of a measure of the thinness of their skin than of the harshness of my column. But that incident and the flash of insight into the real character of the Obama campaign was a harbinger of things to come.

From my ringside seat for the Democrat primary match-up between Obama and Hillary Clinton, it was particularly satisfying to see Hillary's dynastic entitlement machine get utterly torched—for the first time. That her crown was getting smacked off her head by an upstart Democrat out of nowhere with a Muslim name made it all the more delicious. And nothing was more satisfying than watching the red-faced rage building in former president Bill Clinton, who for some elusive reason fancied himself as "America's first black president."

One of the most revealing moments about the Clintons came in South Carolina after Obama eviscerated Hillary by thirty points. Bill Clinton, the fornicator in chief, responded the way Democrats so often do when their backs are against the wall. He pulled out the race card and played it as vigorously as he could.

Attempting to marginalize and racialize Barack Obama and his stunning victory over Hillary Clinton, Bubba invoked another failed politician—who just happened to also be black. "Jesse Jackson won South Carolina in '84 and '88," he sniffed to reporters in Columbia. "Jackson ran a good campaign. And Obama ran a good campaign."

It was as condescending as it was despicable. It was so bad that my editor and I wondered to each other whether Clinton was intentionally sabotaging his wife's campaign. As a buddy of mine at the time noted, if Hillary were elected president, she would go down in history as America's first woman president. Bubba would be left as a footnote, known as a lecherous ex-president who boffed an intern in the Oval Office. Intentional or not, watching the Clintons blow themselves up and get destroyed in the Democrat primary made it very hard for me to not like Barack Obama.

Now to be clear, a liberal Democrat from Illinois was never going to be a candidate that I would vote for. But going back to Obama's speech at the 2004 convention, he was singing a different tune—a very fundamentally pro-America tune. He spoke of the importance of parents and families and how the government cannot read to children at night. That was a breath of fresh air from a Democrat. He offered a very unifying and patriotic vision. Again, we are talking about 2004, when Obama was still peddling "hope" everywhere he went. Also helping him was that he had zero record. While I was cautiously skeptical, everything I knew about him sure beat the hell out of the Clintons. And it is certainly true that his being black had everything to do with his soaring success, or, as Bill Clinton would later call it, the "biggest fairy tale I've ever seen."

Anyway, we at the *New York Post* gave Obama a fair shake.

And then along came the Reverend Jeremiah Wright.

Wright had been the Obamas' pastor at Chicago's politically connected Trinity United Church of Christ for the better part of thirty years. He officiated at the Obamas' wedding and baptized both of their daughters. He was a firebrand.

Excerpts of some of Wright's incendiary sermons leaked to the press in early spring of 2008.

He talked about America's chickens coming home to roost, called America the "No. 1 killer in the world." He said we deserved the 9/11 attacks and harangued about "white folks' greed." Wright also talked about "them Jews" controlling everything and warned of "white racist DNA" running through people's brains. In one memorable sermon, he hollered: "U.S. of KKK A!"

It was as if he were running for racist in chief.

All of it was, shall we say, a wee bit off script from the sunny, positive, hopeful campaign Barack Obama had meticulously crafted. To be sure, Wright's comments were incredibly racially prejudiced and divisive, fairly dripping with hatred, not to mention the jubilant espousal of reckless and irresponsible conspiracy theories about AIDS and Jews and the like.

Furthermore, politically speaking, it certainly was no way forward for America in terms of continuing the extraordinary strides toward equality we have enjoyed over the past fifty years.

"White folk done took this country," Wright fumed in one sermon. "You're in their home and they're gonna let you know it. You are not now, nor have you ever been, nor will you ever be a brother to white folk and if you do not realize that you are in serious trouble."

Understandably, there was considerable outrage when the sermon quotes from a Chicago church bled into open political discourse on the national stage.

But I have to tell you I had a slightly different view of it all. I looked around at all my fellow political reporters—overwhelmingly white, Ivy League educated, and from big cities in the North—and I just had one question. My goodness, have any of you ever been to a black church?

Black churches in the South—especially in the rural South where I grew up—are pretty genial affairs. But there is still plenty of fire and brimstone and when the preacher gets rolling, he tends to lay it on the line. If you are a white guy sitting in a pew—no matter how joyously you were welcomed at the start of church—you will likely find yourself squirming a little at some of the high points of the sermon.

When I was in Detroit as a reporter for the *Detroit News*, I worked Sundays. In my search for stories, I logged as much time as I could going to the big churches. Never have I been more welcomed than at those big black churches. But when the preacher got to listing all the injustices in this broken world, he never flinched from putting a fine point on things. It was always the same villain: "the man." And he was always the same color: white.

After the sermon, everybody—1,500 black congregants and

this one white guy—all went back to getting along just fine and hugging and shaking hands and slapping backs. The preacher had his say. Everybody hollered back in approval. And then we all got back to getting along. In all of its awkwardness, it is kind of how Americans have always successfully moved along on our journey to a more perfect union.

Ironically, I thought one of the wisest things about the nature of black churches was something Jeremiah Wright himself said: "Barack Obama's a politician. I'm a pastor. We speak to two different audiences."

Still, it was pretty disgusting stuff that Barack Obama's personal preacher had been spouting for a long time. Even more so since it had all spilled into the political arena. Needless to say, if a white politician's preacher had made similar comments about blacks or Jews or the conspiracy theories, all hell would have broken loose and the politician would most likely have been drummed from public life. Can you imagine, for instance, if Donald Trump's personal preacher of thirty years had said such racially incendiary things?

The Obama campaign had worked so hard to craft this positive image of Obama as unthreatening and hopeful and welcoming. He, of course, denounced the comments of his preacher. But then he did something that surprised everyone. The campaign hastily gathered those of us traveling with the press into a small auditorium across from Independence Hall in Philadelphia, the nearly sacred ground known as "the Birthplace of the Nation," where the Declaration of Independence was adopted on July 4, 1776.

In a speech he titled "A More Perfect Union," Obama began by quoting the preamble to the U.S. Constitution. He once again denounced many of Wright's quoted statements.

But he also admitted that, indeed, he was well aware that his longtime preacher had delivered the fiery political diatribes, even racially scorched ones, that were the most controversial. More brazenly, Obama also refused to condemn the man himself and told us bluntly:

"I can no more disown him than I can disown the black community. I can no more disown him than I can my white grandmother—a woman who helped raise me, a woman who sacrificed again and again for me, a woman who loves me as much as she loves anything in this world, but a woman who once confessed her fear of black men who passed by her on the street and who on more than one occasion has uttered racial or ethnic stereotypes that made me cringe.

"These people are a part of me," Obama said. "And they are a part of America, this country that I love."

It was, for sure, a brave speech. Not your usual political bromides. I admired it immensely. The speech, I thought, revealed a man who understood all the worrisome complexities of race and our troubled history and yet remained singularly focused on pressing forward toward "a more perfect union."

I am a white guy who grew up in the rural South. I have always read about families "torn apart" during the Civil War. That was not my family. Every drop of blood that my family shed during that awful conflict fell in the service of the Confederacy. There were no divisions in my family. The stories of their heroism in battle were passed down to all their descendants and remain cherished today.

I feel no need to apologize for my forebears. Nor am I so arrogant as to second-guess their wisdom in deciding to fight for their state of Virginia instead of the Union.

I was also raised by very good parents and grandparents

who taught us that all people are equal in God's eyes, no matter what. And no matter their skin color or anything else, all people better damned be equal in our little eyes. If we ever mistreated anyone for any reason whatsoever, there would be hell to pay. They, too, yearned for "a more perfect union" and bequeathed to us that same profound desire.

But still. A white guy from the South. A son of Virginia, the very capstone of the Confederacy. It can be hard to live like that in a world where everything is a bumper sticker and history gets emotionalized and perverted into some crazy social justice campaign. Your only hope is that somebody—especially those who lead us—understands all the strange complexities of race and our troubled history, yet remains singularly focused on pressing forward toward "a more perfect union." In this context, those who would use racism to divide us deserve a special place in hell.

When I left Independence Hall that day, I was convinced Barack Obama was a truly rare, honest politician with integrity who was capable of leading this great country with malice toward none and charity for all.

Boy, would I—and so many Americans—be profoundly disappointed.

The wisdom I thought I saw that day in Philadelphia turned out to be cheap glitter. The decency I detected turned out to be a cold shiv in the back. His depth of understanding was as shallow as it was insulting. He would turn out to be nothing more than another craven politician blowing with the wind.

The first clue came a few months later just as he was finally clinching the Democrat nomination. Suddenly all his great principle that had required him to stand with his racist preacher evaporated. He held a press conference in South

Dakota to announce that he was ditching Jeremiah Wright and quitting his longtime church.

A cynical person might question the timing.

Did Barack Obama stick with his nasty old black preacher while he was still wooing black voters in the Democrat primary? Did he ditch the black preacher once he began to turn his attention to the general election, where the fiery preacher would be less politically beneficial—perhaps even a liability?

I can't be certain, but it sure seemed like page one out of the playbook the Clintons and the Democrat Party have used for decades. And we would not have to wait for Barack Obama to become president to see the race card played again.

A few months later, in August, Republican nominee John McCain aired an ad attacking Barack Obama's celebrity status among the dewy-eyed media. Though the ad was considered "innocuous" by some for slamming Obama as "famous for being famous; he's more flash than substance," others were ready and waiting to pounce, with race card in hand.

The *New York Times*, always eager to do Obama's dirty work, issued an editorial charging the McCain campaign of running a "racially-tinged attack." Why? Because the ad compared Barack Obama—a black man—to Britney Spears and Paris Hilton, two white women.

You cannot make this stuff up. But these are the people who have ordained themselves the arbiters of all that is racist in America today. The *New York Times* sparked a brush fire. An online blogger popular on the left accused McCain of running "crypto-racist ads." Another TV wag shilling for the Obama campaign at the time said McCain's ad was "deliberately and deceptively racist."

Another Obama toady named Josh Marshall wrote on

the Internet that the McCain campaign was pushing "the caricature of Obama as an uppity young black man whose presumptuousness is displayed not only in taking on airs above his station but also in a taste for young white women."

What? I am not sure which is worse: Marshall's obsession with finding racism where it does not exist or his bizarre fantasizing about Barack Obama and his "taste for young white women." Either way, he probably should stick to lurking around his favorite peep houses instead of attempting political commentary—even if it is only on the Internet.

The occasion of Obama's election as America's first actual black president triggered a media orgy of navel-gazing introspection about matters of race in this country nearly 150 years after the Civil War. Most of it was ridiculous and over-the-top. For the Great White Media, Obama really had become the messiah.

And speaking of Obama as the messiah, I was reminded of my travels with the Obama campaign in 2008, when various fellow travelers regularly referred to the 757 that ferried us around the country as "Messiah One."

Who needs the U.S. Air Force when you are a deity?

As meteoric as Obama's political rise was, he was remarkably bad at retail politics. He exuded a certain disdain for other people and never seemed to particularly enjoy being around them. For a politician, he was an odd duck.

Returning from his world tour aimed at burnishing his nonexistent foreign policy record, I pestered the campaign to grant me an interview with him. Eventually, they did, and somewhere over the Atlantic between Berlin and the United States, I was ushered through the Secret Service section to the front of the plane, where Obama's private cabin was.

I do not recall much of the interview and I don't think I got anything particularly earth-shattering out of it.

But I was struck by how unpleasant and unmannerly Obama was. He and Robert Gibbs were seated across from each other at a table when I entered the room. Neither budged.

"Okay," I thought. "So I will stand here."

When I offered my hand to shake, Obama paused, as if he was not going to shake my hand. After a few beats too long, he finally lifted his hand—still seated, of course—and gave me a limp, dead-fish handshake without even looking in my eyes.

Now, I couldn't care less, of course. But I could not help but register Obama's small, petulant little gesture. Later, after I got kicked off the campaign plane, I was hardly surprised by the thin-skinned sensitivity.

Still, the historic milestone of his election was certainly cause for celebration. And it marked a pretty good point to stop and reflect on our rough history and how we got to that moment—even for those of us who were not particularly enthusiastic about Obama's politics.

Slavery, racist Jim Crow laws, and segregation had all passed away long before. We survived the civil rights movement. It was a mighty struggle but, thankfully, we got there together. Even more remarkable were the waves and waves of changes in people's personal attitudes over the generations. I am not talking about petty prejudices that inform—rightly or wrongly—every living, thinking human being on the planet. I am talking about actual, ugly, back-of-the-bus racism.

Well before America elected her first black president, racism had been hounded to the farthest fringes of American society. Anyone in a position of power who ever demonstrated racist prejudices would not remain in power long. Think about it. What is the worst thing that can be said about anybody today? What is the one thing that will end your political career in an instant? Destroy you in Hollywood overnight? Cause you to lose your job tomorrow? Being labeled a racist. That is a testament to the soaring success of people like Martin Luther King and so many others.

By the time Barack Obama arrived on the political scene, America had never been more unified in her rejection of racism.

Of course, this success does not come without problems. When devious actors in the media or politics redefine "racism" to mean whatever they want it to mean, they can then use that powerful weapon to destroy any enemy they pick. So toxic is the mere notion of being tarred as a racist that many good people—myself not included, obviously—go to great lengths to avoid even discussing race, in public or in private. The risk is just too great that one stupid comment or unintentional slip-up could ruin you.

This is certainly not a healthy way for a big, diverse, and rowdy family of 325 million to get along in any honest way.

Anyone in America hoping for a healing respite from the racial demagoguery of politics, once President Obama got elected, would soon be disappointed. It would not take Obama long to put away his sunny rhetoric about hope, his fake Greek columns and pablum about racial unity, once he was inaugurated.

Early in his first term, Obama went on a global apology tour, visiting places like the Middle East to apologize for America. It was ironic that he was in a place riven by intractable racial and religious discord, yet he was apologizing for a great nation built upon principled ideals of liberty and dedicated to all people being equal, regardless of race or religion. He told an audience in Cairo that it was "part of my responsibility as president of the United States to fight against negative stereotypes of Islam wherever they appear." This was the tone Obama set.

Back home, things were no better. The month after Obama's apology tour, police in Cambridge, Massachusetts, arrested a man who was breaking into a home after neighbors called 9-1-1. It turned out the subject who got arrested was a black Harvard professor, Henry Gates Jr. He was breaking into his own home after the front door got jammed shut. And neighbors, suspecting someone was breaking into Gates's home, called police.

Inexplicably, America's first black president, only months into his first term, decided to jump into the middle of the controversy—a hot mess already being spun by the media as racially motivated.

"I don't know, not having been there and not seeing all the facts, what role race played in that," Obama told reporters, before launching into the whole fiasco displaying all of his ignorance and accusing the cop of being a racist.

"I think it's fair to say, number one: any of us would be pretty angry. Number two: the Cambridge police acted stupidly in arresting somebody when there was already proof that they were in their own home. And number three: I think we know separate and apart from this incident is that there's a long history in this country of African Americans and Latinos being stopped by law enforcement disproportionately."

As Obama's term progressed, his fixation with race became more evident and more politically divisive. Over at the Department of Justice, he installed Eric Holder, who later boasted that he operated as the president's "wing man," as opposed to being an independent attorney general for the

United States. In many ways, Holder was the tip of the sword for President Obama's racializing political agenda.

One of Holder's first moves as AG was to quash a major voter intimidation case that career prosecutors had put together against members of the so-called New Black Panther Party. In this case, two members of the New Black Panther Party—one of whom was a certified poll worker—stood guard outside a polling station. One was carrying a billy stick and both were hurling racial epithets at white voters.

Much of this was caught on video and the case was fairly clear-cut. Democrats have long claimed to be the party willing to fight tooth and nail against voter suppression. But Holder and Obama killed the case. Apparently they were concerned about the suppression of certain voters, but not others—if you know what I mean. The indefensible decision sent a startling message to career staff inside the Department of Justice—as well as the country as a whole. At Justice, Holder and Obama aimed to keep their thumbs on the scale.

Scrapping the case against the New Black Panthers was only the beginning of an eight-year campaign by Holder and the Obama administration to position the Department of Justice against the very men and women helping enforce the laws: cops. This was especially true when anything came up with cops involving race. As with the Cambridge police officer, it was always the cops who were said to be at fault.

The Justice Department also took sides against Immigration and Customs Enforcement at a time when Democrats were desperate to curry political favor with Hispanic voters. As Democrat political machines in big cities around the country declared themselves "sanctuaries" for illegal aliens to hide from federal immigration authorities, Holder had their back.

To be fair, it wasn't just in matters of racial politics that Obama's Justice Department sought to tip the scales. Holder also refused to prosecute IRS officials for targeting political enemies. He became the first attorney general in history to be held in contempt of Congress for his strenuous efforts to cover up numerous scandals inside the Department of Justice.

Even after Holder left, the department would continue to be weaponized by refusing to prosecute Hillary Clinton for her email scandal and, we would later learn, launching a major spying operation into a political opponent's campaign at the height of a presidential campaign.

Back at the White House, President Obama kept the fires of racial injustice stoked. Among the more frequent guests to the White House was none other than Al Sharpton, perhaps the most shameless race hustler in America. He is breathlessly celebrated in the media despite his lifelong efforts at sowing racial division and his key role in the heinous case of Tawana Brawley's rape hoax allegations against four white men, including a prosecutor and two cops.

Perhaps unsurprisingly, "post-racial" America after Obama is pretty ugly. That is because it is anything but "post-racial." In fact, it is far more racial and divided than at any time in a generation. Widespread polling revealed a steep decline in racial harmony during Obama's presidency.

"Our latest poll suggests that far from healing America's racial wounds, the first black president has reopened them," *Investor's Business Daily* reported in 2014. "Obama the uniter is actually the great divider."

By a three-to-one margin, Americans said race relations deteriorated under Obama, according to the poll. Nearly one in four said relations have gotten "much worse." Who could have possibly imagined such a development with Al Sharpton on the scene?

The images on television were even more discouraging. Full-fledged riots broke out in Ferguson, Missouri, and Baltimore during President Obama's second term. Both were in response to police action against black suspects.

In Ferguson, a white police officer shot a black man after the man lunged into his squad car and tried to grab the officer's gun. Among Democrat politicians in Washington, this aggressive move from a guy who had just roughed up a store clerk and stolen a box of cigars became known as "Hands up! Don't shoot!" Among the ringleaders of this gross distortion was Sharpton himself. Democrat politicians in Washington were right behind him ready to pour more gasoline on the fire. Members of the Congressional Black Caucus—a segregated club in Congress—took to the House floor with their hands up and gave speeches in solidarity with the thug who assaulted the officer and appeared to have been trying to murder him.

In the midst of the riots, President Obama dispatched his attorney general, Eric Holder, to the scene. Al Sharpton was already there. Naturally, Holder launched a Justice Department investigation into the police department. Despite all the political hysteria, a grand jury of Missouri citizens later determined that the officer did nothing wrong and acted in self-defense. The subsequent federal investigations found that the black suspect had neither put his "hands up" nor even said "don't shoot." The Department of Justice determined that the officer acted lawfully and was merely defending his own life.

Democrat politicians take pride in being the party of so-called racial identity politics, claiming it is important to represent each group of disenfranchised victims. They run campaigns overtly designed to fragment voters into camps based on race, gender, religion—anything they can find to divide people—and then pit them all against one another in an election.

Remember the Republican so-called war on women? Or Hillary Clinton's ridiculous "I'm with her" campaign motto? President Obama's "wise Latina" Supreme Court justice? In truth, all of it is racial or gender profiling, something they claim to be vehemently opposed to. In any other business it would be called what it really is: racism.

There are two reasons Democrats wage this kind of overt racial politics.

First, it is extremely effective. There is no more potent weapon in politics today than to accuse your opponent of being racist. It not only destroys your enemy, it silences him. Professional Republicans live in terror of being called racist. Often, such as in the case of illegal immigration, Republicans will vacate the battlefield of an important issue even before Democrats have trundled out their tired old "racist" weapon.

This is also why Democrat politicians like to racialize every issue. If they can make it about race, then they automatically hold the upper hand, especially against timid Republican politicians. Again, consider illegal immigration.

It is why they even racialize crime. Especially crime. All they need is a black defendant and they can make the whole thing about race. And, of course, the media dutifully follows right along.

There is a second reason Democrat politicians are so wedded to racial politics. By making everything about race, they avoid any debate or scrutiny about the actual policies they are pushing on the people they claim to care so much about.

It is why they make everything from housing to poverty rates to crime all about race. Because if all these problems are not caused by race, then perhaps they are caused by all the policies that have been put in place by the Democrat politicians.

The idea, for example, that black-on-black crime in cities run entirely by Democrats is somehow evidence of racism is simply a lie. That is not to say it is not a terrifying problem. It is. It's just not racism.

Barack Obama certainly did not invent racial politics. But he sure exacerbated it during his eight years in office.

The riots in Missouri were so bad and bled so deeply into the fabric of America that people began talking about the "Ferguson effect." It was all a result of Democrat politicians trying to politicize an awful criminal situation for political gain. It instilled widespread disrespect for police, which in turn caused police officers to question how effectively they really should be doing their jobs. Why arrest someone if it risks your winding up being accused of murder? Or even worse, a racially-motivated murder?

This was never more evident than when riots broke out in Baltimore the following year when a black suspect died after a bumpy ride in the back of a police van. Amid the fires and mayhem, six Baltimore cops were arrested, including three black cops. After all the Democrat politicians were done making as much political hay as they could out of the tragic situation, cooler heads prevailed. All the cops were either acquitted or all charges dropped.

The "Ferguson effect" also thrust the so-called Black Lives Matter movement onto the national political stage. At its best, the movement highlights the real tragedy going on in American cities today, where alarming numbers of black men are violently killed every year. But even this, in the hands of Democrat politicians, gets weaponized into something racial, as if racism were somehow killing all these people.

Democrat fixation on the racial politics of crime was never more awkwardly obvious than when Hillary Clinton—running for the Democrat nomination in 2016—spoke at a black church. She told a story about a lesson she learned from her mother about treating people kindly. Clinton concluded by declaring that "all lives matter."

This drew immediate groans from people sitting inside Christ the King United Church of Christ. Making Clinton's offense even worse, the church she was visiting was just a few miles from Ferguson, Missouri, where the black suspect killed by a cop had (not) put his hands up and had (not) said, "Don't shoot!"

By the time Clinton's comment made the political rounds, she and her campaign were in pure meltdown. There was only one thing to do: bow at the altar of racial politics. She later issued a correction and declared that, in fact, all lives don't matter. "Black Lives Matter."

Meanwhile, over in the Republican primary, something else had taken center stage. His name was Donald Trump. And, unlike just about anybody in politics—especially Republican politicians—he couldn't give a rat's ass if you called him a racist, or anything else. Not that he is remotely racist or condones any form of racism.

As he himself told one interviewer: "I am the least racist person you have ever interviewed—that I can tell you."

Trump just doesn't care that his enemies try to hurt him by accusing him of racism. He is simply impervious to the all-powerful "racist" weapon that Democrats have been deploying for so long against anybody they want to destroy or silence.

Illegal aliens from Mexico who are "rapists." The "Muslim ban." Third-world countries Trump calls "shitholes." For Democrats—and the dutiful media—this was all resounding evidence that Trump is a racist. Of course, most rational thinking Americans do not believe this. They heard the same things and thought Trump was talking about illegal immigration, radical Islamic terrorism, and third-world countries. And people roared their approval of a guy in the public spotlight who finally stood up to the race bullies and said *Enough!*

Early in the Republican primary, the media tried pinning white supremacist David Duke to Donald Trump, demanding that Trump "disavow" Duke after Duke made positive comments about Donald Trump.

Why CNN would hang around listening to a racist like David Duke is a mystery and would bear investigation by the Southern Poverty Law Center if they themselves were not such a corrupt organization. Anyway, CNN's Jake Tapper was demanding that Trump declare independence from David Duke.

"Honestly, I don't know David Duke. I don't believe I've ever met him. I'm pretty sure I didn't meet him and I just don't know anything about him," Trump responded.

Trigger media meltdown. Trump was not finished.

"I don't know anything about what you're even talking about with white supremacy or white supremacists. So, I don't know. I don't know—did he endorse me or what's going on?

Because I know nothing about David Duke. I know nothing about white supremacists."

To the media, this just proved Trump really was a racist. But to regular people, it actually proved that for the first time, a guy stood up to the race bullies and refused to play along with their racist little games. Trump would not even agree to the terms of discussion Jake Tapper laid out.

Even more enraging for the media, Trump gallingly offered to do some research and get back to them. He would look up David Duke and whatever group he supposedly represents that no decent person has ever heard of.

"I'd have to look," Trump said, pretending to be helpful. "If you would send me a list of the groups, I will do research on them and certainly I would disavow if I thought there was something wrong."

Not only is Donald Trump a racist, the media concluded, he is a lying racist. All because he refused to play along with their perverted games. The evidence that he was lying came in the form of a statement back in 2000 that Trump had made to the *New York Times*. Explaining why he quit the Reform Party, Trump noted the membership of David Duke, "a Klansman."

Ah-hah! This proved that Donald Trump, in fact, did know who David Duke is and lied about it!

No, actually, it simply proved that Trump was not about to play some reporters' twisted game geared to smear Trump as some kind of racist. It only proved that Trump publicly quit the Reform Party because he did not want to be associated with "a Klansman," which seems like a fairly unracist move.

As the media was breaking out in hives over Trump's obvious racism, voters were breaking out in cheers that somebody was finally standing up to the race bullies.

As the record shows, the media went straight to calling Trump a racist right out of the gate. They screamed it again. They screamed it more. They screamed it about everything.

And, yet, Trump persisted.

Donald Trump refused to lie down, defeated by their accusations. Democrats and the media had never seen anyone impervious to this—their most powerful weapon. Nobody in politics had survived even one of these circuses. But Donald Trump just kept on going. Soon enough, Democrat politicians and the media decided to circle back and try reinventing their weapon with updated terminology and more complex explanations for why and how everything Donald Trump said and did was racist.

He is a "white nationalist." Okay, we might be onto something here. Trump is definitely a "nationalist." And he is "white." So, you know, okay, Donald Trump is a white nationalist.

Well, they ventured, if he is a "white nationalist," then that means he is part of the "alt-right."

What? What the hell is the "alt-right"? Turns out the "alt-right" is yet another term made to accuse someone of being racist in cases where there is no evidence whatsoever of the person actually being racist.

When all else failed, they accused Trump of playing racist "dog whistle" politics, meaning that he is secretly sending secret messages to secret voters that—like a dog whistle— cannot be heard by the regular human ear.

Oh. My. Goodness. These people keep getting dumber and dumber. If there is just one thing you learn about Donald Trump, it should be this: Donald Trump does not do "dog whistle." There is nothing "dog whistle" about him. Donald

Trump is a straight "bullhorn" kind of guy. He says what he is thinking, completely unfiltered. There is nothing silent about his blunt message.

All of the attempts to smear Donald Trump as a racist fell flat. It was all a giant waste of time and verbiage. Even with all the new words and terms, Donald Trump still did not care that Democrat politicians and their handmaidens in the media were hell-bent on sliming him as a racist.

He just kept motoring on and people cheered him all the way.

Probably the most painful moment of the Trump presidency was that haunted weekend in the late summer of 2017 in which an innocent woman was killed when she was run over by some racist nut from Ohio who drove his car into a crowd in downtown Charlottesville.

It was painful because a young woman got killed. Two Virginia state troopers trying to keep the peace also died that weekend when their helicopter crashed. Painful, too, was the bullhorn that got handed to a bunch of racists spewing their hateful nonsense. And, as always happens in these situations, the whole thing got distorted and politicized beyond recognition by Democrat politicians and the media.

For decades now, Virginians have debated Confederate monuments. We have done so peacefully. Everybody gets together. Everybody says their piece. Sometimes people get a little worked up. But people do not normally come to blows over the monuments to the Confederacy.

Sometimes the monuments are taken down or moved elsewhere. Sometimes names get changed or monuments are altered. Sometimes they just remain. It is a tricky balance between people venerating their brave ancestors and being respectful of fellow Virginians who might take offense at the memory of such a painful history.

It bears noting that many of the people involved in the Charlottesville fiasco were, of course, not from Virginia.

But it all began innocently enough as a debate over the statue of Robert E. Lee in what was then called Emancipation Park in Charlottesville. Previously, the park had been known as Lee Park until the city council voted that summer to change the name. Still being decided was what to do with the statue of the great Confederate general that graces the park. Like many Confederate statues, it was cast and erected in the early 1900s after the South had begun to recover from the economic ruins of the Civil War and Reconstruction.

Like many statues around the state of Virginia, this one had been a topic of increasing debate in recent decades. I have witnessed these debates as a citizen. I have covered them as a reporter. And I have witnessed them as a consumer of the media. And I can tell you with all certainty that, indeed, there are good people on both sides of these debates. Sure, there are nasty people, too. There are nasty people on both sides. But there are certainly good people on both sides.

As soon as the media gets involved and the politicians start to feast, all truth and sanity goes right out the window. Early on when Trump's critics could not make their "racist" weapon work against Trump, they invented new words and terms to try smearing him. "Alt-right." "White nationalist." But these did not stick, either.

"I am the least racist person you have ever interviewed— that I can tell you," Trump said more than once.

Whenever the Great White Media descends on some town in the South to cover a fracas about a Confederate flag or some monument, they glom on to another invented term, designed to smear and denigrate as racist good people for whom there is no actual evidence that they are racist.

"Neo-Confederate."

What in the ever-living hell is a "neo-Confederate"? Someone riding around out there in 2019 on a horse in the Shenandoah Valley killing Yankees who venture south down Interstate 81? Or, is it someone who tends to his great-grandfather's grave who died in the Civil War? Is it someone who studies the Civil War? Or is it someone who marches around in Confederate garb terrorizing people trying to sleep at night? Or is it someone who is such an enthusiast of the Civil War battles that occurred in his backyard that he takes part in reenactments of those battles? Or is it some toothless yahoo who rides around in his pickup truck looking for people to lynch? Or is it someone who has books about the Civil War on his book shelf?

Well, I am not personally an expert on the term "neo-Confederate," but I have seen it used plenty. And I can assure you that it is an entirely weaponized term used by the media to tarnish as racist all the good people who defend the monuments and revere their ancestors and by happenstance were born in the South.

Donald Trump is the first person to come along in a very long time to give these good people a voice. They are tired of the media distortions about Confederate monuments. They are tired of Democrat politicians trying to racialize everything for partisan political gain. Yet nobody, until a brash-talking Yankee real estate developer from Queens came along, had stuck up for these good people and stared down the race bullies.

So, when asked about the horrific events in Charlottesville, Trump blamed "both sides" for the eruption of violence. This should not have been particularly controversial. In fact, people on "both sides" have since been convicted in court for the violence.

President Trump specifically noted that "you had some very bad people" stirring up violence among those in favor of keeping the Lee statue. But President Trump was not about to allow those racist little miscreants to snuff out the voices of many good Virginians who have always defended the Confederate statues.

"You also had people that were very fine people on both sides," he said.

Which was entirely true. And equally brave to say.

Since the senseless tragedy in Charlottesville, the media and Democrat politicians have only grown nuttier and nuttier when it comes to their efforts to portray President Trump and all his supporters as unreconstructed racists.

They seemed almost delighted when the FBI announced that it had arrested an avowed white supremacist from Maryland for hoarding guns and drugs and who had been plotting a terroristic attack against a list of Democrat politicians and key figures of the left-wing media. But they were not so much delighted that a bad guy had been taken off the streets. Rather, they were delighted that since he had been targeting Democrats, his case would fit neatly into their narrative that, well, Donald Trump is a racist.

One of the more shocking observations came from former Republican National Committee chairman Michael Steele, an advanced sufferer of Trump Derangement Syndrome. In an interview, Steele actually stated that Trump was "probably not happy" that the FBI had stopped a white nationalist from killing a bunch of liberals and media people.

Yikes.

Even stupid stuff becomes supposed proof of Trump's racism.

When the president invited the Clemson Tigers football team to the White House to celebrate their national championship, it happened to be in the middle of the government shutdown. Instead of providing the typically elaborate White House spread, he ordered out for burgers and french fries from fast food-joints for the football team.

Asked if he prefers McDonald's or Wendy's, President Trump was torn.

"I like them all. If it's American, I like it. It's all good stuff, great American food."

To Dan Pfeiffer, a longtime flunky for President Obama, this was somehow proof that President Trump is racist: "Trump patting himself on the back for paying for the cheapest food available for the Clemson Football team after he shut down the government down [sic] is about as Trump as you can get.

"In so many ways, Trump is a racist, angry version of Michael Scott," added Pfeiffer, referring to the popular character from television sitcom The Office.

With people like Pfeiffer making such a mockery of actual racism, it is little wonder that race relations deteriorated so much under President Obama.

It is not just President Trump who is the racist. All of his supporters are, too.

Hollywood idiots refer to the red "Make America Great Again" hat as the "new white hood."

The *Washington Post* published a column from a professor comparing the red hat to a Ku Klux Klan hood or robe. Wearing one "constitutes a deliberate political act and deliberate provocation."

The *Post*'s fashion critic Robin Givhan also got in on the red hat hysteria, explaining: "To wear a MAGA hat is to wrap oneself in a Confederate flag. The look may be more modern and the fit more precise, but it's just as woeful and ugly."

Is it any wonder that deranged anti-Trumpers out there are incited to violence against people wearing these hats?

And is it any wonder that HBO soap opera actor Jussie Smollett used the MAGA hat in the elaborate hoax he staged in order to get a pay raise from the creators of his show?

So, where and who are the true racists in our society? Well, some of them are scattered throughout the land—sad, hateful people, often misfits and nearly always lacking the smarts and sophistication to have any impact on our nation's rocky march toward a more perfect union. Any threats they pose are immediate and specific—certainly nothing capable of contaminating our society.

Far more dangerous than these scattered bigots are the smarmy political sophisticates who live and breathe their passion to control the electorate. Armed with vast banks of computer-generated polling and personal information, emboldened by pretentious arrogance, these wretched politicos harness their high-octane deceit to slice and dice voters into little niches of people who can then be pushed one way or the other with information that is often false. Essential in this process are religion and gender and racial ethnicity—always the raw ingredients of racism.

With great cunning, swathed in callous indifference to what's good for the nation, these political operators are able to create and sustain loyalties among voters, as well as bitter divisions. In every sense, these geeks and the political parties who are their masters are the true racists in our society.

Voters can be quickly forgiven for not understanding how all of this works. But in their guts, they know they have in President Trump a man who probably doesn't understand it, either, and wants nothing to do with it.

★CHAPTER FOUR★

VERY STABLE GENIUS

There's a new muttering around town that has become the mantra of the Never Trumper Republicans as well as the media elites who long for their old comfort zones in covering the president. "This is not normal," they say. Those most deeply afflicted with Trump Derangement Syndrome repeat the mantra as if they could erase the past three years by just repeating it over and over again like a political rosary.

"This is not normal."

I hear it from political reporters who are still shell-shocked, wandering dazed through the rubble wondering what the hell came out of the clear blue and knocked them all down like a shell blast.

Dan Rather says, "This is not normal."

Ex-President Obama, who paved the way for the Trump presidency, says, "This is not normal."

Countless newspapers and magazines covering national politics have devoted entire articles to the repeated mantra, "This is not normal."

President Trump at his desk in the Oval Office
(Official White House Photo by Shealah Craighead)

One electronic political rag on the Internet ran an entire story titled "This is Not Normal," beneath a picture of President Trump on the telephone in the Oval Office, Andrew Jackson peering down above a bucking-bronco bronze sculpture by Frederic Remington.

The story itself was fourteen paragraphs long and consisted of the same sentence written over and over and over again. Four hundred and forty times.

"This is not normal."

The article concluded with this: "You're absolutely correct. None of this is normal."

Sometimes I find myself jubilant watching these people consume themselves with anger and rage. They despise Donald Trump so much it is hard not to love him just on those grounds alone.

He is like kryptonite to them. Electing him president was like pouring an entire shaker of salt onto a slug. They writhe in pain, begin frothing until they turn inside out.

If I wind up going to hell, I am pretty sure it will be because of how much I enjoyed watching all these people writhe in such misery over Donald Trump.

While on the topic of "normal" and "not normal," it bears consideration of what is actually not normal.

Owing $22 trillion in debt is truly not normal. It also should not be normal for legislators to steal from government programs aimed at keeping the poor and elderly from starving and throwing that money away on other government boondoggles.

Forcing taxpayers to put money into government-run retirement accounts—and then stealing that money to spend on other purposes. That is not normal.

And, of course, if anybody other than the federal government did any of these things they would be thrown in jail for the rest of their lives.

Just ask Bernie Madoff.

To many Americans, here are some other things that are not normal:

Leaving all three major entitlement plans on a glide path to insolvency within a generation is not normal.

Passing a bunch of laws and then not enforcing them is not normal.

Maintaining a hopelessly porous border that we do not defend is not normal. Thinking that it is okay that more than ten million illegal aliens have invaded our country in violation of our laws is not normal.

Running around the world using our sophisticated military to enforce other people's borders while ignoring the invasion at our own border is really not normal.

Truth is, at the end of the day, the federal government has just a few simple responsibilities that cannot be taken on by anyone else. The first is to defend our borders. As valiant and dedicated as our Border Patrol and Immigration and Customs Enforcement are, they cannot do it alone. They especially cannot do it while politicians in Washington constantly carp about them, undermine their work, and create uncertainty about what they are supposed to be doing. Describing these brave men and women as Nazis and comparing detention facilities for illegal aliens to concentration camps and threatening to abolish ICE is as cruel to those men and women risking their lives every day as it is counterproductive to the overall mission.

As for Congress, they have one huge and overriding mission above all others and that is to use the power of the purse. Their biggest job—and theirs alone—is to simply approve twelve appropriation bills to fund all the departments of the federal government. Now, we can argue about how many of those departments should be eliminated and how many more should have their budgets slashed like households or small businesses in America do during tough times. But at the moment we have twelve departments that need to be funded and so Congress needs to approve spending bills for each of them.

Astonishingly, President Trump's first full year in office was the first time in ten years that Congress passed appropriation bills on time for the president's signature. This kind of disregard for basic budgetary processes and disdain for taxpayers tells you all you need to know about professional politicians in Washington today. Of course, this refusal to follow fundamental spending rules is why Congress passes all these massive, pork-laden, opaque "omnibus" spending bills. It is also why we see so many government shutdowns.

None of this is normal, yet it has been around for decades and was growing worse and worse long before Donald Trump ever got into the White House.

Meanwhile, the *Federal Register,* the daily publication from the National Archives that makes available to the public the rules, regulations, and other legal notices issued by federal administrative agencies, is also an informal measure of how much bureaucratic nonsense is being heaped upon the innocent taxpayer. You will not be surprised that it keeps getting larger and larger.

President Trump's first year in office was a banner year for Americans who want limited government. Only 61,950 pages were added to the *Federal Register,* according to the Competitive Enterprise Institute. *Only!* That was the lowest number of pages added to the *Federal Register* in a quarter century.

President Trump's first year in office also saw the lowest number of new rules added to the *Federal Register* in the forty-plus years those records have been kept. The good news is that among those 3,281 new rules, many actually repealed previous rules that had been added under previous Congresses and previous presidents.

This was a massive blow to the federal bureaucracy in just one year. President Obama's last year in office saw the largest number of pages added to the *Federal Register* with 95,894 pages, adding 3,853 new rules.

So, if you want to talk about what is truly not normal, I will grant you that Donald Trump is not your run-of-the-mill Washington politician. In that respect, he is not normal. And that is precisely why he got elected.

It doesn't really bother me how much the political press in Washington hates Donald Trump. They are entitled to their opinions. I don't even care how wildly out of touch they are with regular Americans out there who are paying all the bills. What bothers me is how dishonest and deeply delusional they become when they try covering Donald Trump as compared to their coverage of other politicians.

"He's a narcissist!" they scream. "All he cares about is himself!"

Seriously? Are you freaking kidding me? Have these people ever interviewed a politician before? Did they just fall off the back of a turnip truck and find themselves covering politics in the capital of the most powerful nation on earth?

Did they read any Machiavelli in school? Do they get Netflix? Ever watched *House of Cards*?

Honestly, you don't need to turn to fiction or television or even sixteenth-century Italian political literature to understand the breed of people drawn to politics. They are all narcissists, at least to some degree.

The first thing you learn covering Congress is why all the hallways are so wide: So they can accommodate the massive ego of members of Congress walking up and down them.

One of President Trump's favorite techniques on Twitter is to refer to himself as "your favorite president."

In the summer of 2018, after his former lawyer Michael Cohen had his office raided, for instance, President Trump tweeted: "Inconceivable that the government would break into a lawyer's office (early in the morning)—almost unheard of. Even more inconceivable that a lawyer would tape a client— totally unheard of & perhaps illegal. The good news is that your favorite President did nothing wrong!"

Cue the hysteria.

Never mind that a president under a sprawling—and questionable—investigation had issued a comment about a raid by federal agents of his own personal lawyer's office, which included tapes of conversations between the president and his former lawyer. We are talking a major constitutional situation and all anyone could talk about was how outrageous it was that Trump would refer to himself as "your favorite President."

It is yet another example of reporters being simply incapable of catching on to Donald Trump's humor. Any normal person in America saw that line and burst out laughing.

Realizing how crazy it makes all the right people, President Trump trolled again when he issued a "Hold the Date!" tweet announcing a big Independence Day bash.

"We will be having one of the biggest gatherings in the history of Washington, D.C. on July 4th. It will be called 'A Salute to America' and will be held at the Lincoln Memorial. Major fireworks display, entertainment, and an address by your favorite president, me!"

Hilarious, right?

Not for these folks. More hysterics accusing the President Trump of denigrating the holiday and usurping patriotism for his own political needs.

As usual, Bill Kristol—founder of the *Weekly Standard* magazine and Trump Derangement Syndrome—summed up the hysteria perfectly. "The last president to try to hijack July 4th was Richard Nixon, who staged Honor America Day on July 4, 1970. It was widely ridiculed. Nixon later left office in disgrace."

So, you get that? Trump throws a big party for the nation on the Fourth of July and is accused of *hijacking* the national holiday—an "offense" so serious that his term may end in a Nixonian disgrace. It is simply preposterous.

Aside from their inability to find their own funny bones, swamp reporters also are completely incapable of evaluating the veracity of simple statements President Trump makes.

But first, it must be noted, that—again—we are talking about politicians practicing politics. And they are shocked—*shocked*, I tell you!—to find gambling going on. Holy crow, have these people ever listened to a single political speech in their lives? Politicians make stuff up all the time. In fact, they do it so much that most reporters give up on trying to report all the little lies.

After all, what is the definition of a scandal in Washington? When a politician accidentally tells the truth. Such scandals are relatively rare—because it is so seldom that anybody around here tells the truth.

Yet President Trump says anything with the slightest twinge of bull and suddenly it's Watergate all over again. Exhibit A will always be the president's boasting about the size of his inauguration crowd. Not since the Pentagon Papers has anything out of Washington gotten so much press coverage. (*Warning*: In case any political reporters are reading this, that line is what we call "hyperbole." Kind of a joke, but trying to make a point.)

Vogue magazine became so consumed with President Trump's supposed "lies" that they published a list of his twenty-five biggest on the occasion of the two hundredth day of his administration. The list is extraordinary, revealing just how wildly jaundiced—not to mention, unfunny—political journalism has become in these times.

Among the top "lies" noted by *Vogue* were a series of presidential tweets in which Trump described how anti-Trump MSNBC hosts Joe Scarborough and Mika Brzezinski had begged to visit his Mar-a-Lago resort in Florida.

Twittered Trump: "She was bleeding badly from a face-lift. I said no!"

The magazine acknowledged that, indeed, Scarborough visited for dinner one night and the couple returned for another visit the next night. And, in fact, Brzezinski was, in fact, recovering from cosmetic surgery. The lie? The magazine claimed that the lie was that Trump did not actually turn the couple away.

Another "lie," according to the magazine, was when President Trump said former FBI director James Comey was not respected inside the agency and referred to him as a "showboat," perhaps one of the funniest things Trump has ever said about an enemy. The magazine's evidence that this was a lie? A quote from another senior FBI official who said that "the vast majority of FBI employees enjoyed a deep, positive connection to Director Comey."

That quote, and I am not making this up, was from former acting FBI director Andrew McCabe, who was eventually fired for lying.

The list goes on and on and on with moronic claims like this. It reaches full-moon absurd when it fact-checks the president's defense of his son in the midst of some media-manufactured "scandal."

"Don is, as many of you know, Don, he's a good boy. He's a good kid."

"In fact," *Vogue* reported in all seriousness, "Trump Jr. is a 39-year-old man, and father of five."

Dear Lord, we do not deserve to keep this republic!

Politico magazine, so deeply concerned about the effects of President Trump's "lying," wrote a very serious story about the psychological effects on people who are constantly being lied to. Obviously, they should have conducted a reader survey if they simply wanted the answer to that question.

Instead, they recounted more and more supposed "lies" and interviewed a bunch of professors for their article titled "Trump's Lies vs. Your Brain."

"Our brains are particularly ill-equipped to deal with lies when they come not singly but in a constant stream, and Trump, we know, lies constantly, about matters as serious as

the election results and as trivial as the tiles at Mar-a-Lago,"
Politico reported, referencing a claim Trump supposedly made
about how Walt Disney himself crafted the tiles in the nursery
at Mar-a-Lago.

"When we are overwhelmed with false, or potentially false,
statements, our brains pretty quickly become so overworked
that we stop trying to sift though everything," the magazine
concluded. "It's called cognitive load—our limited cognitive
resources are overburdened."

Lord, help us.

Reporters pride themselves on having keen and sensitive
"BS detectors," we call them. Like a spider lying in wait at
the corner of her web, she senses the slightest vibration of
dishonesty and pounces. Well, certainly a BS detector is a very
important thing to have. The only thing worse than having
a broken BS detector that never rings is having a broken BS
detector that never stops ringing. And that is where we are with
political journalism in Washington today. That's how all those
the little fibs and boasts and funny asides from President Trump
wind up as front-page fodder in once-serious newspapers.

President Trump's real sin is that he is an outsider. He is
not a professional politician. He is not one of them. Even more
vulgar is that he faithfully represents voters whom these people
have deep disdain for. The people who elected Donald Trump
are a bunch of dumb, toothless, racist rubes, in their minds.
Such people are to be lied to and double-crossed by politicians
once they get elected. The politicians aren't actually supposed
to keep the promises they made to those unwashed, hard-
working folks who elected them.

Add to that President Trump's flamboyant and
confrontational style and you have a real skunk at the garden

party. Take his tweeting habit, which the president relies on to get his message out directly to the people without it getting perverted by the media. Between his election and Inauguration Day, reporters spilled barrels of ink worrying about whether Donald Trump would keep up his tweeting in the White House.

In the first place, of course he would! Why on earth would he surrender such a vital tool for communicating directly with the American people? In the second place, the only reason these people wanted Trump to quit was that they didn't like him in the first place. They don't like his style.

Nothing, of course, sparks pearl-clutching vapors among the political press the way President Trump does when he mixes his unorthodox manners and rodeo-style humor with a touch of self-effacing bravado. And, every time, nitwit reporters and late night so-called comedians reveal their own angry obtuseness, as when Alex Baldwin scrunches up his dirty lips, squints, and totally misses the joke. Everybody else knows that Trump is never funnier than when he is extolling his own considerable virtues.

The media went perfectly mad when, during an event with supporters in Ohio, President Trump declared that he is "non-braggadocious" as he proceeded to take credit for the thrumming economy.

"You know, you can work hard, but if you don't have the right leader setting the right tone—in all fairness," Trump said, catching himself, "I'm not even saying. I am non-braggadocious."

As usual, Trump brought the house down with that one. And the media went mad.

Not as mad, of course, as when then-candidate Trump celebrated Cinco de Mayo—thumbs up—by boasting that the

Trump Tower grill made the best taco bowls. That was, to the unfunny press, apparently racist or something.

But nothing—and I mean nothing—topped the President's Twitter musings after about one year in the White House.

"Actually, throughout my life, my two greatest assets have been mental stability and being, like, really smart," he thumbed. "Crooked Hillary Clinton also played these cards very hard and, as everyone knows, went down in flames."

I could not find any evidence of this, but I bet somewhere, some reporter "fact-checked" this statement and determined that Hillary Clinton did not, in fact, catch on fire at any point during her campaign.

But the president was not finished.

"I went from VERY successful businessman, to top T.V. Star to President of the United States (on my first try). I think that would qualify as not smart, but genius . . . and a very stable genius at that!"

Needless to say, the Internet. Melted. Down.

But Donald Trump is not just noodling reporters and his detractors when he issues his "non-braggadocious" yet hilariously self-effacing Twitterisms. He is also being the master marketer he has been all his life. It is the secret to his success in real estate, in building golf courses and skyscrapers and in keeping relevant inside the pages of the New York City tabloids. And, of course, it is the secret to his success as a "T.V. Star." President Trump is never more than about five sentences away from branding himself or whatever it is he is selling. Stay on message. Constantly remind people who you are, what you are selling, and why your product is exactly what people need.

During the Republican convention in Cleveland, Trump

scandalized the political world when he promised to bring real change to Washington.

"I have joined the political arena so that the powerful can no longer beat up on the people who cannot defend themselves," he said to roars of approval. "Nobody knows the system better than me, which is why I alone can fix it. I have seen firsthand how the system is rigged against our citizens, just like it was rigged against Bernie Sanders—he never had a chance."

It was a line Hillary Clinton would later seize upon during her convention speech in Philadelphia. Her problem? Trump said: "I alone can fix it." To her, this meant Trump was not trustworthy. The news media fell right into line and roasted Trump for the comment.

"Breaking with two centuries of political tradition, Donald Trump didn't ask Americans to place their trust in each other or in God, but rather, in Trump," was the headline used by one magazine.

For somebody like Donald Trump, such criticism is not just silly, it is self-defeating. If you are offering yourself up to do a job and you are not the only person qualified to get the job done, then why are you running for office?

It is a question, apparently, that never occurred to the Clintons in their twenty-five years terrorizing the national political scene.

Perhaps an even better way to understand just how much contempt these lazy reporters have for President Trump is to consider their everyday coverage of him, as compared to other politicians who have served in recent times in Washington.

Imagine, for instance, if Donald Trump had once belonged to the Ku Klux Klan. Do you think that would be a story? How long do you think he would have lasted in public office if he had once been an officer in the Ku Klux Klan? Well, I can tell you that Senator Robert Byrd of West Virginia was most definitely in the Ku Klux Klan and to this day he holds the record for being the longest-serving senator in U.S. history. For more than fifty-one years, Byrd served in the august United States Senate as a Democrat, having previously served as Exalted Cyclops of the Ku Klux Klan. And when he finally quit office, Byrd was not run out on a rail, tarred, and feathered by the Trump-hating media. The only reason he left office in 2010 was that he died.

Or, consider this. What if President Trump had left a boozy party near his vastly wealthy father's family compound, drove off a bridge, and turned the car over in the water. Instead of rescuing the young woman who was riding with him, he got himself out and fled. Instead of immediately calling for a rescue, he slinked home in a rowboat to concoct a web of lies in order to protect his political future. How long do you think Donald Trump would last if the media found out he did something like that? Well, if his name was Kennedy, he would last in public office more than forty-five years. And like Exalted Cyclops–turned–U.S. senator Robert Byrd, Ted Kennedy would only leave office due to death.

What if President Trump went into heat over an intern working for him *in the White House while he was president*? What if the intern was barely the age of consent? Much younger than his own daughter. What if he and his cigar had repeated illicit relations with the young woman while his wife was in the residence?

What if he then proceeded to lie about the whole thing and then concocted an elaborate scheme to make the young, impressionable intern and his secretary lie to a federal grand jury about the whole affair? How long do you think President Trump would survive if he did something like that? While in office?

Or, how about this one? What if Donald Trump gave an attractive nineteen-year-old intern a "personal tour" of the White House. The teen was a virgin, at least before the tour. "Haven't you done this before?" he asked, to which she replied, "No." He proceeded "more gently." And when he was done, he pointed her to the bathroom.

This, of course, was not Donald Trump. It was the King Creep of Camelot, the vaunted, revered, and still-beloved John F. Kennedy, assaulting a teenage intern moments after meeting her and conducting his vile business among the paintings and busts of his own children.

That heinous episode—only revealed in recent years— was positively romantic compared to what he made the poor, nineteen-year-old girl do later, when the two were splashing around in the White House pool, the tiles of which can still be seen in the basement below today's White House Briefing Room.

Kennedy aide David Powers was sitting on the edge of the pool, pant legs rolled up, lolling his feet in the water. The president of the United States slithered up to his intern and said, "Mr. Powers looks a little tense. Would you take care of it?"

"It was a dare," the teen later recalled. "But I knew exactly what he meant. This was a challenge to give Dave Powers oral sex. I don't think the president thought I'd do it, but I'm ashamed to say that I did."

As if that were not repulsive enough, JFK then surrendered all pretenses of being anything other than a lowlife dirtbag: "The president silently watched," the teen recalled.

Of course, Kennedy would go on to be assassinated in Dallas, which preserved the myth of Camelot, as if in amber, to never be questioned or doubted. The dishonest myth would extend to Kennedy's little runt brother, Teddy, and an infestation of the whole Kennedy clan in American politics for a half century.

Yet, somehow, the political press reserves all their disdain and indignity for Donald Trump.

In their gargantuan sense of entitlement, they actually believe that Donald Trump is unfit, simply because they do not like him and his style. He is not Camelot, no matter how disgusting and lecherous "Camelot" actually was. And because they despise Trump, he should be eliminated from politics.

★CHAPTER FIVE★

*President Trump with newly confirmed Supreme Court Justice Brett
Kavanaugh* (Official White House Photo by Joyce N. Boghosian)

IN TRUMP'S COURT

For a half century now, American self-governance has been under relentless, coordinated assault by a cabal of leftist establishment politicians hell-bent on destroying the republic the Founders fearlessly envisioned, painstakingly fashioned, and ultimately bequeathed to us. With a deep and undeniable affinity for socialism and unmistakable strains of totalitarianism, these modern-day Marxists aim to destroy the closest approximation of justice and equality ever known on earth. They want to replace it with a demonic dystopia where equality is replaced by government-picked winners, where individual freedom is squelched by the cultural whims of the state, and wealth is quashed by welfare.

The godfather of this crusade was a scalawag promoted by liberals as the "Lion of the Senate." Edward M. Kennedy was the runt child of the American political family that came to wealth and power in the early twentieth century. Senator

Kennedy began this assault on America in 1962, seven years before he killed Mary Jo Kopechne on Chappaquiddick, an island a few miles from his family's compound on Cape Cod in Massachusetts.

Though Ted Kennedy shared the celebrated licentiousness of the entire male Kennedy clan, he was nonetheless considered the dumbest of the whole lot. Horny, stupid, and without regard for human life is a pretty rough mix. The only way to get through life with that toxic combo is if your daddy has lots and lots and lots of money. Mob connections help, too.

When I first began covering Ted Kennedy, he had been retired to the U.S. Senate after a failed political career on the national stage. In those days, Kennedy could be found almost every day in what we called "Lower Senate Park," just across from the old Russell Senate Office Building, where his main suite of offices was located. Several times a day he would be out in the park, throwing a tennis ball to his beloved Portuguese water dog.

Throughout the Capitol, that dog was treated like royalty. There was no place the dog could not go. His name was—and I am not making this up—"Splash." Yes, as in the sound a 1967 Oldsmobile makes when it careens off a bridge and lands in the water upside down with a twenty-eight-year-old woman trapped inside, who agonizingly suffocates to death after the thirty-seven-year-old driver has fled the scene in order to concoct a story to protect his own political future.

Like I said, it's a lethal mix: horny, stupid, and no regard for human life. Add to that a profound sense of entitlement and it's like splashing gas onto a fire.

Emboldened in spite of these dubious qualities, Ted Kennedy still thought he should be president. But even

Democrats around the country understood that Teddy's glib charade would not work anywhere outside of his home state of Massachusetts, where voters were still wallowing in the afterglow of President John F. Kennedy, Teddy's older brother, who was assassinated in 1963. Teddy permanently proved his damaged-goods label in 1980 during his final, spectacular face plant on the national political stage when he lost in the primaries to Jimmy Carter.

Prior to that, political scientists believed such a feat as losing to Jimmy Carter was impossible—especially for a pretty face named Kennedy. But, as has been noted, Ted Kennedy was born on third base and stole second base before getting thrown out on first.

But the Massachusetts Senate seat—the same seat held by his illustrious brother, JFK—was his. It would take something even worse than his lies about the death of the girl in his car to hound him out of it. So, with no other future prospects, Kennedy was left to carry out his demonic visions from his comfortable perch in the U.S. Senate—not a bad perch at all. Kennedy was always a club man, so in that respect Congress was the fanciest club he could join. Few clubs reward licentiousness, stupidity, and arrogance more handsomely than the United States Senate.

But, with Ted just one of one hundred, the task of destroying the American spirit would take a lot of schmoozing and a lot of ball-tossing in the park to Splash, and the process would take that much longer. But Kennedy and his cabal of dedicated anarchists were in it for the long game. Most important, they seemed to be having fun.

ALIENS AND JUDGES

In order to carry out their assault on the American spirit, Kennedy and his cronies chose a two-pronged attack—each of which would subvert the clear will of the American voter. If successful, they would radically alter the landscape not just of the American political world, but of just about every aspect of American life.

Already, in his Immigration Act of 1965, Kennedy had prepared the way to usher into the country a steady stream of unskilled foreign-born people. These people, once given a front seat at the public trough and registered to vote as faithful Democrats, would advance the agendas of Kennedy and his elites. The bill abolished the quota system—which limited the number of immigrants that could come from various regions of the world—and allowed naturalized citizens to sponsor relatives in what would be known as chain migration. Skilled workers had previously been exempted from the quota, but subsequent reforms put highly skilled workers in a newly designed preference system.

The other prong of attack was more subtle and far more insidious—one that would extend the kleptocratic hand of the federal government more deeply into every aspect of American life. Kennedy and his cohorts must have cackled with delight as they envisioned their end run around the voters by hijacking the unelected federal judiciary.

In 1973, the Supreme Court, in one of the most controversial rulings in its history, had provided a spectacular example of how courts can accomplish rules that could not be accomplished through traditional legislative channels. The key to it, of course, is a very loose interpretation of the Constitution. In this case, the Constitution says not one single word about abortion. In fact, the Founders could not have imagined legalizing such a medical procedure, let alone found some constitutional protection for it.

Yet, in the landmark case *Roe v. Wade*, the highest court in the land—a bank of unelected justices—found a constitutional right guaranteeing unfettered access to abortion. This right, they ruled, emanates from "the penumbras" of the Fourth Amendment's right against unlawful search and seizure. Left unexplained by the majority's 7–2 ruling was whatever happened to an unborn citizen's right against a brutally lethal search and seizure. But, whatever.

According to these robed arbitrators, this constitutional right to abortion was found in "the penumbras"—the eerie shadows around the ghostly light of a half-lit moon. In other words, it is an optical illusion—an optical illusion good enough for the black-robed arbiters to set the stage for millions of legal abortions across the land—all without a vote of a single representative of the people.

As controversial as this unquestioned edict by the high court is today, it was even more shocking and controversial back then. Gallup's polling at the time found support for abortion around 46 percent—hardly the kind of groundswell to get such a proposition pushed through the elected members of Congress.

Today, when you step back and put *Roe v. Wade* into the larger "arc" of justice in America, I can see how the Supreme Court might have ruled in that case that an unborn child had a constitutional right to life. That is the kind of right the Supreme

Court is supposed to protect. But I will never understand how the court found this supposedly Constitutional right to extinguish the life of an unborn child.

In the forty-five years since that ruling, legal scholars across the entire political spectrum—and, specifically, both sides of the debate about abortion—have found that the majority ruling in *Roe v. Wade* is a disaster of legal thinking and could not possibly withstand genuine and rigorous scrutiny by any legitimate court of American legal scholars.

As rickety as the ruling is for federal judicial precedent, it has been even more corrosive in American politics. Here you have a court of unelected judges declaring by fiat some constitutionally guaranteed right floating in "the penumbras" that no ordinary, commonsense voter could imagine. And by forcing that odious ruling onto the American people, the Supreme Court ripped the hot-button issue out of the hands of voters and the elected legislatures and arbitrarily and capriciously gave it a status beyond any mortal appeal.

But the high court had ruled. Therefore, voters and the legislature were supposed to shut up and obey.

Where common voters saw judicial overreach and a terrifying mockery of constitutional rights (not to mention contempt for the sanctity of life), Ted Kennedy and his fellow travelers were warmly inspired.

Borking Robert Bork

The next major highlight in Ted Kennedy's jihad against an impartial, nonpartisan federal judiciary came in July 1987 after President Reagan nominated the unquestionably qualified federal judge Robert Bork to replace retiring Supreme Court justice Lewis Powell. Though Judge Bork had previously been widely respected for his judicial experience and temperament, he had crossed into the world of the most vicious and dishonest political attacks by being named to succeed a sitting justice known for being the "swing vote" on the Supreme Court.

This, of course, represented the same threat liberals saw in the nomination of now–Supreme Court justice Brett Kavanaugh. Because Kavanaugh was nominated to replace "swing vote" Justice Anthony Kennedy, Senate Democrats and outside left-wing lobbyists inspired by Ted Kennedy's judicial jihad established an entirely new, absurd, and disingenuous standard.

The underlying sin of Robert Bork, and later of Brett Kavanaugh, was that both men as judges believed that the U.S. Constitution is made up of words that have actual meaning. The Constitution—as drafted by the Founders, ratified by the states, and amended by voters over the course of more than two centuries—actually means what it says. The meaning of the Constitution lay not in the unseen "penumbras" of the written document, but in the plain words themselves.

According to the twisted, Kennedy-infected judicial worldview, the Constitution is a "living document." In other words, the Constitution means whatever some unelected federal judge says it means, always based on some predetermined political outcome. It is, without doubt, the most undemocratic, tyrannical, and capricious way to handle the affairs of a free people and settle the disputes of a law-abiding citizenry.

The Founders would be appalled at such a rigged game. But it was the only way Ted Kennedy and his acolytes could transform America into their dream dystopia.

So, literally within minutes of President Reagan's nomination of Judge Bork to the high court, Ted Kennedy took

to the Senate floor to smear the good judge with all manner
of dishonest accusations. In the process, he laid out the entire
strategy for killing the nomination.

Preached the lion of Chappaquiddick:

> Robert Bork's America is a land in which women would
> be forced into back-alley abortions, blacks would sit at
> segregated lunch counters, rogue police could break
> down citizens' doors in midnight raids, schoolchildren
> could not be taught about evolution, writers and artists
> would be censored at the whim of the government, and
> the doors of the federal courts would be shut on the
> fingers of millions of citizens for whom the judiciary
> is often the only protector of the individual rights that
> are the heart of our democracy.

The precise moment that Ted Kennedy became concerned
about the well-being of women in the eighteen years since
he left Mary Jo Kopechne to die in her watery tomb was not
explained. And the reckless and completely unsubstantiated
charge that Judge Bork—or any respected jurist of that day—
wanted to relegate black citizens to the racist laws of the past
revealed only how dishonest and disingenuous the Kennedy
cabal would be. As we saw more than thirty years later with
the nomination of Brett Kavanaugh, these people will say and
do anything to kill the nomination of anyone who refuses to
worship at the altar of leftist judicial activism.

The potency of Ted Kennedy's slanderous speech against
Robert Bork was amplified for two reasons.

First, those were more politically genteel times. Many
Republicans—and even some Democrats—still labored under

the illusion that manners and decency and decorum reigned in the United States Senate, an august body where members are still prohibited from openly disparaging one another or even addressing one another directly during Senate floor speeches. The Kennedy wing of the Democrat Party suffered no such illusions. For them, the Senate floor was the highest parapet from which to launch the most vicious, dishonest—and unanswerable—attacks upon their partisan enemies.

The second massive amplifier of Kennedy's noxious speech against Judge Bork was that just one year before Bork's nomination, the Senate had voted to allow the civics cable upstart Cable-Satellite Public Affairs Network—known as C-SPAN—to begin televising speeches from the Senate floor. Previously, a speech like Kennedy's would have been seen only by a handful of reporters sitting in the press gallery. Only those present would have been able to write an article that would be printed in newspapers the next day.

Ostensibly, Kennedy's slanderous accusations would have been accompanied by some context and allowed Bork defenders to point out that there was simply no evidence whatsoever that Judge Bork wished to bring back segregated lunch counters. But with the message delivered directly to television screens, there was no way to point out that there was not one shred of proof that Judge Bork wanted to relegate black Americans back to being subcitizens. Or that there wasn't even a whiff of evidence that Judge Bork wished young women to die from coat-hanger abortions in back alleys. So the unfiltered remarks went unchecked until newspaper stories were printed the next day or the nightly newscasts aired. And even then, the remarks were so outrageous they took a lot of the oxygen out of the room—as these things usually do.

As stunned as President Reagan and other Republicans were by Kennedy's scurrilous accusations against Bork, they were paralyzed by good manners. For months, the accusations stood, largely unanswered by the White House. The insidious insinuations had plenty of time to sink in and fester and ultimately infect Judge Bork's good name. By the time Judge Bork's confirmation hearings rolled around, it was too late to salvage the man's reputation.

It would be three decades before a Republican president would finally wake up to this kind of vicious assault against constitutionalist Supreme Court nominees. It would be three decades before a Republican president would finally begin fighting back on Kennedy's terms.

Sadly, Kennedy would be dead for seven years before Donald Trump would finally rip out the poison root planted by the "Lion" of the Senate.

GEORGE H. W. BUSH

Among the most deeply addled of the Never-Trump Republicans are so-called "conservatives" who pine for the good old days under the Bush dynasty. That was back when "scandalously inappropriate" meant President George H. W. Bush went out in public wearing loud, bright clashing socks with his smart, tailored suit. That would be the same "conservative" who raised taxes after his famous "read my lips" pledge vowing to never agree to any such thing.

Instead of pushing a supposedly xenophobic, racist "America first" agenda, Bush called for a "New World Order" in which Americans paid dearly to be the world's policeman, gallivanting all over the globe shedding American blood and treasure to fix other people's problems.

And political fights over federal judicial nominations were tamer affairs, handled quietly in the hushed corridors of the U.S. Senate. It was a time when constitutionalist nominees to the federal bench were quietly traded away or diluted by compromise. Or, better yet, Republicans surrendered before even nominating a constitutionalist to the high court.

To be sure, the Bush dynasty deserves credit for some very fine judges on the federal bench. In particular, George H. W. Bush should be applauded for sticking with his nomination of Clarence Thomas to the Supreme Court. Perhaps no other justice on the court was a greater kindred spirit with the late justice Antonin Scalia. And the despicable charade leveled against Justice Thomas by Ted Kennedy and his ilk was as bad as anything leveled against a judicial nominee. At least up to that point.

Likewise, President George W. Bush is celebrated for nominating two fine justices to the high court. Understandably, conservatives felt deeply betrayed by Justice John G. Roberts' ruling basically upholding Obamacare. I have a slightly different view and while his written opinion is clearly and legally indefensible, I understand why he declined to use the power of the Supreme Court to just eliminate Obamacare. His reticence to get involved in the legislative quagmire called Obamacare was entirely based in his deeply-held belief in "judicial humility," something he talked a great deal about during his confirmation hearings.

"Judicial humility" was John Roberts' antidote to "judicial activism," where the federal courts act like unelected Super Legislatures and Super Executives, tearing up laws they don't like and creating new ones as they see fit. In Chief Justice

Roberts's view of "judicial humility," Obamacare was a mess created by Congress and it was a mess that only Congress could clean up. It was not, according to his view, the role of the federal courts to be a Super L-legislature that would step in and tinker with a massive nationalized health -care system that Congress had so unwisely decided to promulgate.

Anyway, if you remove Chief Justice Roberts's ruling on Obamacare, the vast majority of his opinions have been as flawlessly constitutionalist as any justice to sit on the Supreme Court.

Similarly, George W. Bush served the country well by nominating Justice Samuel Alito to the high court. Justice Alito has proven unwaveringly faithful to the Constitution, though it should be noted that President Bush only nominated Justice Alito to the Court after he tried ramming through his longtime friend and lawyer Harriet Miers, who was entirely untested on vital matters of strict adherence to the Constitution.

President Bush should have been particularly sensitive to the dangers of giving a lifetime appointment to the most powerful court in the land to a person like Miers whose instincts as a constitutionalist were unknown. He might have considered that conservatives who care about the Supreme Court have suffered no greater defeat in the past half century than the one delivered by his own father's poor judgment.

When Justice William Brennan retired from the Supreme Court in 1990 after thirty-four years on the bench, conservatives had a rare opportunity to drastically reshape the Court into a more strictly constitutionalist balance. Justice Brennan had been one of the most activist judicial liberals in court history. Though Republicans did not control the Senate, President Bush was enjoying 70 percent approval ratings at the time, according to Gallup surveys. He could have, at the very least, made something of a fight for a constitutionalist nominee for the Supreme Court that conservatives would have loved. He did not.

Instead, Bush chose David Souter, who only that year had been confirmed to the federal Court of Appeals for the First Circuit, based in Massachusetts. Prior to that, Souter had no experience whatsoever on the federal bench. His entire career had been spent serving as a prosecutor and a judge in the New Hampshire state court system. He belonged to the Republican Party. But he belonged to that northeast New England variety of Republican much like George H. W. Bush himself.

Needless to say, Justice Souter quickly entrenched himself firmly in the leftist flank of the Supreme Court, dedicated to expanding the reach of the federal judiciary into every aspect of the private lives of American citizens.

The first instance was in 1992 during *Planned Parenthood v. Casey*, which reaffirmed the *Roe v. Wade* case legalizing abortion. Souter voted in favor of reaffirming abortion rights and sided with Justices Sandra Day O'Connor, John Paul Stevens, and Harry Blackmun. The second decision Souter made that confirmed he was more sympathetic to the left was during *Lee v. Weisman,* in which Souter voted against the right to prayer at a high school graduation.

Justice Souter ruled on the court for nineteen years, retiring in 2009, giving President Barack Obama the first of two vacancies to fill on the high court. Obama would choose as Justice Souter's replacement another liberal jurist, Sonia Sotomayor.

One of the biggest frustrations for conservatives when it comes to filling vacancies on the Supreme Court is that while the courts are littered with terrible judicial activists fecklessly nominated by Republican presidents, Democrat presidents almost never make similar mistakes—at least not in recent times.

President Richard Nixon nominated Harry Blackmun, who became the exceedingly liberal justice who authored the court's majority opinion in *Roe v. Wade*. President Gerald Ford tapped John Paul Stevens, who became a similarly liberal stalwart on the bench. And George H. W. Bush gave us David Souter.

President Reagan was certainly the best Republican president for nominating federal judges over the past fifty years. He elevated William Rehnquist to chief justice and gave us the most forceful conservative jurist of our time in Justice Antonin Scalia. But Reagan's nominees were not without at least some mild disappointment. In 1981, Reagan nominated Sandra Day O'Connor to be the first woman on the Supreme Court. A pragmatist through and through, O'Connor was not a dependently conservative voice for the bench and served as a swing opinion on many cases, including *Planned Parenthood v. Casey* and just about any other case involving abortion "rights."

Democrats, meanwhile, are batting a thousand in nominating liberal, activist judges to the high court. While President Jimmy Carter never got to nominate anyone to the Supreme Court, he did manage to saddle us with Stephen Breyer and Ruth Bader Ginsburg by elevating each of them to federal appeals courts. Following Carter's lead, President Bill Clinton elevated Breyer and Ginsburg to the Supreme Court. President Obama nominated Sonia Sotomayor and Elena Kagan to the Supremes. Not a single one of these nominees got onto the Court and surprised the world by becoming some kind of strict constitutionalist. Each and every one of them has been an eager and reliable proponent of left-wing judicial activism.

GEORGE W. BUSH

Of modern Republican presidents, George W. Bush was among the more sophisticated when it came to judicial nominations to the federal bench. By the time he got elected, conservatives were well onto the game Kennedy leftists were playing with the federal judiciary. Conservatives finally realized the importance of confirming constitutionalists to the courts. They had learned the bitter hard way to scour the writings, rulings, and judicial history of every nominee they supported for the federal bench, from the lowliest district nominees to the Supreme Court. As part of this odyssey, they discovered something else that was powerfully important: youth.

Once all of the jurists who believe courts are a super-legislature are jettisoned, the dark horses with no paper trail are eliminated, and anyone from the school of constitutional relativism has been dumped, one urgent criterion remains: pick them young. The reason is that once you settle on a good, solid, reliable constitutionalist jurist, you want to have them on the bench for a long, long time.

Ironically, George W. Bush's election to the White House should have been a stark lesson for Democrats and liberals about the cruelty of the federal court's intervention in politics. For conservatives, there is no judicial abomination greater than *Roe v. Wade*. In that case, the high court usurped the electoral political process to dictate the most odious and indefensible miscarriage of justice. Even politically liberal jurists today say that the case was wrongly settled. But since it is the product of judicial edict, principled Americans who cherish life and liberty have no recourse or remedy.

Political liberals in America got a taste of their own medicine in the year 2000 when no less than the high court itself stepped in to settle the presidential contest between George W. Bush and Al Gore. However one might argue about the merits of the decision in *Bush v. Gore* versus the court's decision in *Roe v. Wade,* the fact remains: it was the Court settling a political dispute. And no matter how wrong one might think the decision was, there was no electoral remedy available.

Instead of learning a lesson and turning against judicial activism, Kennedy leftists simply doubled down. Even the patriotic unity after the unprecedented terrorist attacks on 9/11 would soon fade away. In short order, Senate Democrats would mount the barricades to combat Bush's federal nominations. By 2003, less than two years after 9/11, a bevy of Bush nominees to all levels of the federal bench had been stalled.

If the Federal City is a hostile place for honest, principled conservatives, it is even more hostile to honest, principled conservatives who also happen to be black or Hispanic or a member of any other group that Democrats divide Americans into and claim ownership of. Some of the most blatantly racist and hostile treatment seen in this country in modern times has been waged against black conservatives in Washington.

Janice Rogers Brown was a judge in good standing on the California Supreme Court—hardly some kind of hotbed of conservatism—when she got pulled into the political meat grinder back east. George W. Bush nominated her to the prestigious U.S. Court of Appeals for the District of Columbia

Circuit, often referred to as the second-highest court in America and often a launching pad for jurists to the U.S. Supreme Court.

When she was nominated, Judge Brown had a sterling reputation, despite her understandable reticence toward government power of any form. Perhaps her most controversial position on the California court had been to harshly rebuke her robed colleagues for taking away parental rights to be simply notified if their underaged child were to have an abortion. During her confirmation hearing, Judge Brown also stated the obvious: that abortion rights—euphemistically referred to in legal circles as "privacy"—were nowhere to be found in the actual Constitution. Of course, they are not. She did, however, during that same hearing confirm that such rights had, in fact, been established by the high court itself.

Judge Brown's deep suspicion of government was understandable. She was born to parents who were sharecroppers living under racist Jim Crow laws in segregated Alabama. Despite those odds, Janice Rogers Brown got an education, earned a law degree, and ultimately ended up on the California Supreme Court. When she got to Washington after President Bush nominated her to the federal appeals court, however, her progress stopped. She was filibustered by Democrats in the U.S. Senate. Even worse, she had to endure insufferable lectures from white Democrats who knew nothing of the grit and wisdom and intelligence that have served Judge Brown throughout her life.

"Let me talk to you for a minute about the world according to you as you see it," Senator Dick Durbin, white Illinois Democrat, lectured during her confirmation hearings. "It is a world, in my opinion, that is outside the mainstream of America."

It was Durbin, not Judge Brown, who was far outside "the mainstream of America," according to California voters. Just a few years before her nomination to the D.C. appeals court, Judge Brown faced California voters on whether to keep her seat on the state's supreme court. A whopping 76 percent of California voters chose to keep Judge Brown on the court. In crazy liberal San Francisco, that vote in support of Judge Brown was more than 79 percent.

In 2014, his last reelection campaign, Dick Durbin mustered a paltry 53.5 percent of the vote in the state of Illinois.

The first and perhaps the most famous of President Bush's judicial nominees to be stymied by unprecedented Democrat filibusters was Miguel Estrada, nominated in 2001 to the D.C. Circuit Court of Appeals. Born in Honduras, Estrada was a sterling immigrant success story. After graduating with honors from Columbia and Harvard universities, Estrada worked for the U.S. attorney's office and Department of Justice. He was widely heralded for his hard work and "towering intellect." No less than Supreme Court justice Elena Kagan, nominated to the high court by President Barack Obama, would later declare that Estrada deserved to be confirmed to not only the D.C. Court of Appeals, but even to the Supreme Court of the United States.

But for Democrats in the United States Senate, there was a glaring problem. Miguel Estrada, they were later caught conspiring in written memos, was "Latino." And he was being backed by the "wrong" people—meaning principled conservatives.

In 2003, I was covering judicial nominations for the *Washington Times* when a reliable source of mine called to tell me that a batch of highly explosive memos written by Democrat staffers on the Senate Judiciary Committee had been discovered after staffers had left them on an unsecured staff computer server. Clearly spelled out in the memos was the conspiracy among Democrats on the Senate Judiciary Committee to block the nomination of Miguel Estrada specifically because he was Hispanic. In the memo to Dick Durbin, staffers openly argued that Estrada was "especially dangerous" because "he is Latino."

Democrat opposition to Estrada was further intensified because they viewed him as a potential pick for the Supreme Court. At the time, he would have made history by being the first Hispanic on the high court. Working closely with outside lobbyists opposed to Bush's judicial nominees, Democrats on the Judiciary Committee plotted their effort to block Estrada. In a memo dated November 7, 2001, a Durbin staffer recounted a meeting Durbin had missed with Ted Kennedy and the outside lobbyists.

"[Y]esterday's meeting focused on identifying the most controversial and/or vulnerable judicial nominees, and a strategy for targeting them," the Durbin staffer wrote. "They also identified Miguel Estrada (D.C. Circuit) as especially dangerous, because he has a minimal paper trail, he is Latino, and the White House seems to be grooming him for a Supreme Court appointment."

Democrat opposition to Estrada over his "minimal paper trail" is particularly ironic considering liberals' supposed opposition to holding Hispanics living in the United States responsible for a lack of documentation. Why wasn't Estrada merely "undocumented" in their eyes? Why did Democrats have to oppose him simply because he had a "minimal paper trail"? Or was it just because he was a "Latino" who might be destined for the Supreme Court?

When I confronted Durbin over the astonishing admission of racism in their effort to block Estrada, he refused to condemn the plot. Instead, he only complained that the dastardly memos never should have been revealed to the public. He claimed that smoking-gun emails had been "stolen." Eventually, after I reported on the racist plot, staffers for Durbin claimed that the memos failed to capture just how un-racist Democrats on the Senate Judiciary Committee actually were. Estrada was "dangerous," they argued, because he was "Latino"—in a good way. Meaning that being Latino was such a positive attribute for Miguel Estrada that it would make it difficult for them to oppose him and therefore he should be filibustered.

In other words, in Democrats' racial purity, they had loved Miguel Estrada too much. They loved him to death.

Welcome to Washington politics.

Anyway, as if that made any difference to Estrada. Whether it was because Democrats hated Hispanics or loved them, Estrada was being filibustered by Democrats because he was Latino. By any definition of "racism," this would certainly qualify. For Estrada himself, it certainly did. And, in 2003, after more than two years of being filibustered, Estrada withdrew his nomination and returned to private practice. Senator Ted Kennedy issued a jubilant press release declaring it "a victory for the Constitution."

Sean Rushton, an outside advocate working to get constitutionalist judges confirmed to the federal courts, saw the treatment of Janice Rogers Brown and Miguel Estrada quite differently from the way Kennedy saw it.

"With Miguel Estrada, and again in [the case of Janice Brown]," he told me at the time, "we see a highly qualified lawyer who is an ethnic minority and who happens to be conservative again being blocked. There's a real pattern here that seems to establish a Democrat double-standard for conservatives who happen to be ethnic minorities."

It wasn't just qualified minorities that Democrats worked furiously to keep off the federal bench. The secret memos also revealed how they actively sought to stack certain judiciary panels in order to rig the outcome of certain cases being decided by the courts. In one such case, Democrats on the Senate Judiciary Committee conspired to block the nomination of one of President Bush's nominees to the Sixth Circuit U.S. Court of Appeals until after that appellate court decided on two major affirmative action cases dealing with the University of Michigan and its law school.

In 2001, George W. Bush nominated Judge Julia S. Gibbons, a respected constitutionalist judge from Tennessee, to a Cincinnati-based court—the same year U.S. district judge Bernard Friedman ruled that the admissions policy at the University of Michigan clearly had racial motivations similar to a quota system. The case went to the Sixth Circuit and Democrats revealed in those memos that they wanted to delay a conservative nominee to the court until the decision had been decided.

"The thinking is that the current 6th Circuit will sustain the affirmative action program, but if a new judge with conservative views is confirmed before the case is decided, that new judge will be able, under 6th Circuit rules, to review the case and vote on it," staffers wrote.

The plot worked out exactly as Democrats hoped. While Judge Gibbons was eventually confirmed on a 95–0 vote to the appeals court, it was not until after the Sixth Circuit ruled in favor of upholding the affirmative action programs at the University of Michigan and the law school. But their underhanded victory would be short-lived. In a blow to Democrats' unstinting efforts to inject race into every corner of American life, the Supreme Court later decided to take up the Sixth Circuit's perverted ruling on affirmative action. The high court reversed the lower court and affirmed that racial quotas as used by the University of Michigan were illegal, but that race could be a consideration for admission for a time. The majority opinion ruled that race should be a time-limited admissions factor and eventually phased out.

With President Bush, constitutionalists had the best advocate in the White House since President Reagan. But in the 2000 election, voters also delivered a grievous blow to Republicans in the U.S. Senate. Going into the election, the GOP held an eight-seat advantage, 54 to 46. This advantage was entirely wiped out by the election, leaving the Senate teetering on a 50–50 tie. This meant that for the first three weeks of January 2001, Democrats held control with Vice President Al Gore holding the tie vote as president of the Senate. After Bush's inauguration, that tie vote would go to Vice President Dick Cheney.

But given Republicans' flawless record for screwing up, they soon lost even that slim advantage when on May 24, 2001, Senator Jim Jeffords, a Vermont "Republican," abandoned the party and became an Independent who caucused with Democrats. This left Republicans at a 51–49 disadvantage, meaning—crucially—that Republicans lost the chairmanship of the Senate Judiciary Committee. Democrats took full advantage of Republican misfortune and began blocking President Bush's judicial nominees, even after eight years of President Clinton's nominees piling up inside the federal courts.

As maddening as all this was, what happened next—
after Republicans regained control of the Senate—was even
more infuriating. In 2002, President Bush bucked history by
picking up seats in his first midterm. Republicans gained two
seats in the Senate and eight seats in the House. This kind
of cushion would give Republicans plenty of room to move
judicial nominees out of the Senate Judiciary Committee.
It also meant that those nominees would generally go to
the Senate floor with majority support. But Democrats had
other ideas. Presurred by outside special interest lobbyists,
senate Democrats broke with history and began for the first
time filibustering routine judicial nominees who had the full
support of a majority of the U.S. Senate. In other words, senate
Democrats were thwarting the clear intent of the Constitution
by using parliamentary tricks to prevent the senate from
confirming a president's judicial nominees even though they
had a majority in the US Senate.

This made Democrat filibusters of Janice Rogers Brown,
Miguel Estrada, and Julia S. Gibbons unprecedented.

The only reason Democrats had this power to thwart
such qualified nominees who had clear support from the
full Senate was the arcane, tradition-bound rules of the U.S.
Senate. Nothing in the Constitution stipulates anything about
giving any minority in the U.S. Senate the right to undermine
the will of the full Senate when it comes to confirming the
president's judicial nominees. Or when it comes to anything
else, for that matter. But those were the rules that the Senate
had agreed to at the formation of every new Senate every
two years going back decades or longer. As conservative
frustrations grew both inside the Senate and among outside
observers over these Democrat filibusters, some began

talking about changing the Senate rules to remove the sixty-vote threshold for confirming judicial nominations.

Senator Trent Lott, Mississippi Republican and former leader of the Senate, had confidently told me of a "nuclear option"—a parliamentary maneuver that could be deployed to clear the unprecedented backlog of qualified constitutionalist nominees. This would entail a bare majority of the Senate (meaning just 51) voting to change the rules so that nominees could be confirmed on a straight up-or-down vote. It was such a dangerous and secret idea that Lott referred to it as "nuclear." And, of course, the fallout inside the cordial and collegial Senate would be "nuclear" as well. As if there wasn't already plenty of "nuclear" fallout left by recalcitrant Democrats who were clearly straining the rules and violating the clear will of the U.S. Senate in their effort to corrupt the federal judiciary.

So, what did Republicans wind up doing? Did they employ the "nuclear option"? Did they bring sanity to the U.S. Senate? Did they take advantage of their majority control of the chamber to advance the installation of principled constitutionalist judicial nominees to the federal bench?

Of course not.

Instead, a band of the weakest Republicans abandoned the supposedly conservative party and formed with Democrats the insidiously named "Gang of Fourteen"—seven members on each side—to try to prevent the nuclear option. The idea was that the seven Republicans would vote against the nuclear option as long as the seven Democrats voted to proceed on considering some of the filibustered judicial nominees. In the end, it was a negotiation with Democrats that broke the logjam of Bush's nominees and confirmed a handful of them to the positions for which they were nominated.

Even though Republicans had all the control they needed to confirm every last one of the nominees, they still agreed to kill some of the nominations that Democrats and their outside lobbyists were most opposed to. Those sacrificial nominees were some of President Bush's most constitutionally principled nominees.

At this point, three of the nominees had already withdrawn their names from consideration and five of the seven remaining were confirmed. Both Henry Saad and William Myers were denied an up-or-down vote. Saad was denied due to Senator Harry Reid's concerns about his national security background (a violation of Senate rules) and Myers was denied due to alleged anti-environmental views.

All of this acquiescence by Republicans was done in the name of keeping the peace in the United States Senate. Sadly, yet predictably, Democrats had no intention whatsoever of keeping the peace once they regained power.

Of course, none of the shady backroom dealing was any solace to Miguel Estrada, who had already abandoned his nomination after two years of waiting—and all because he was Latino. Perhaps most maddening of all was that part of the disgusting sellout deal with Democrats stipulated that President Bush would get certain nominees confirmed—on the condition that he never nominate them to a higher bench. Janice Rogers Brown, the splendid jurist who was born to sharecropper parents in segregated Alabama, was one of those dealt such an insulting blow. Democrats agreed to place her on the D.C. Court of Appeals so long as Republicans agreed to never nominate her to any higher court.

Aside from being a craven abandonment of principle, the deal struck me as entirely unconstitutional as well. What right does anyone—even a sitting U.S. president—have to make any deal that curtails a president's power to nominate anyone he chooses to any position in the federal judiciary? That is a power reserved for the president and the president alone. No one—and especially not some gang of deleterious Democrats or soft-spined Republicans in the U.S. Senate—should have the power to undermine that executive power.

Republicans may have been too timid to deploy the nuclear option. But—as was predicted at the time—when Senator Harry Reid, Nevada Democrat, gained power over the Senate in 2007, he would have no such weak-kneed hang-ups. Reid invoked the nuclear option in 2013, meaning only a simple majority was needed to pass judicial nominees. He did not apply the rule to Supreme Court nominees, mostly due to concern that Republicans would weaponize that power in the future, which, of course, they ultimately did anyway.

Conservative disappointment over judicial nominations under George W. Bush did not end there. In addition to leaving fine jurists such as Miguel Estrada and Janice Rogers Brown wounded on the field, the Bush years saw a decidedly spotty record appointing solid justices to the Supreme Court. When Supreme Court justice Sandra Day O'Connor announced her retirement, it was an opportunity to replace a mild constitutionalist with a more principled one. President Bush nominated federal judge John G. Roberts, a darling of Washington establishment conservatives. But before confirmation hearings could get under way, tragedy struck. Supreme Court chief justice William H. Rehnquist—one of the greatest constitutionalist stalwarts of the past half century—died. Bush withdrew Judge Roberts's nomination to replace O'Connor and renominated him to replace Rehnquist as chief justice. Suddenly the stakes were so much higher.

Over strenuous opposition from Democrats, Roberts would get handily confirmed by the Senate. Since then, much has been made about Chief Justice Roberts's deciding vote in 2014 to uphold Obamacare. But anyone who sat through Roberts's confirmation hearings should have been able to predict exactly how a Justice Roberts would come down on that case. Despite the outcome of that particular case, Roberts's adherence to a strict philosophy against judicial activism was clear. Throughout the hearings, he called it "judicial humility" and he was clearly committed to it.

But in the case of the Obamacare ruling, it was pretty harsh medicine to take. Roberts's written opinion seems unprincipled and indefensible but his message was absolutely clear. The other two branches of government were resoundingly clear that they wanted a massive new federal program to take over the health industry in America. If the American people wanted to undo that effort, they would have to do it at the ballot box. The federal courts were not going to do it for them.

This ruling was certainly in keeping with Roberts's view of "judicial restraint." It was also his effort to salvage the reputation of the federal courts, which for far too long had exhibited undue interference in the deepest recesses of American life. Still, many constitutionalists were outraged that a Republican president and a Republican Senate would nominate and confirm a chief justice who would later cast the deciding vote to uphold Obamacare—the greatest big-government assault on freedom in America in modern times.

After getting Roberts confirmed to replace the great Chief Justice William Rehnquist, President Bush and his establishment allies were mighty pleased with themselves. This was still nine years before Roberts's ruling on Obamacare, and the strict constitutionalists who had dutifully supported President Bush for eight years were pleased. Their loyalty had paid off. But, still, it was something of a draw. In the best case, replacing Rehnquist with Roberts simply maintained a safe constitutionalist seat. Replacing a swing vote like Sandra Day O'Connor was a pickup opportunity for conservatives. Or, at least, it was something of a half pickup. And thanks to a growing effort inside organizations such as the Federalist Society, a solid bank of young, principled constitutionalists had been identified to help Republican presidents pick good judges and justices who wouldn't turn hotly activist as soon as they were given lifetime jobs on the federal bench. No more David Souters! President Bush had a long list of good people to choose from whose background, writings, and rulings had been thoroughly vetted.

He ignored them all.

Riding a wave of pride over Chief Justice Roberts's confirmation, President Bush picked a friend—his own lawyer—to be on the high court. Harriet Miers was a loyal friend to President Bush. She was from Texas but had become a blue-chip member of the Republican establishment in Washington. But she had never operated as anything other than a lawyer. She had never ruled on a case. She had no discernible judicial philosophy. She was, at best, a complete unknown.

Democrats, obviously, were tepidly optimistic at the massive blunder by Bush. Harry Reid said the Court would benefit from a lawyer without judicial experience and more time spent actually practicing law. Senator Chuck Schumer said the pick could have been worse. Senator Dianne Feinstein was also optimistic. As enthusiastic identity-politics Democrats, they were predictably pleased with the fact that Miers was a woman.

Conservatives were rightly horrified. "Souter in a skirt!" they declared about the entirely untested Harriet Miers.

Here was a simple opportunity after decades of frustration and defeat at the Supreme Court to install a true constitutionalist to the bench. A Republican was in the White House. Republicans controlled the Senate. It was an easy win. A lay-up. And in his arrogance, Bush picked a buddy from the old establishment network. It proved everything principled conservatives hate about establishment Republicans in Washington.

The outcry was as vicious as it was predictable. At first, Republican senators went through the motions, agreeing to meet with Miers. But as time went on, with conservatives around the country who care about the integrity of the high court and who have learned the lessons of running with dark horses and blank slates, Republican ranks in the Senate began to break.

Eventually, the White House realized they had no hope of getting Harriet Miers confirmed. The stakes were too high and Miers was too unknown. At her request, Bush withdrew her nomination and returned to the drawing board in search of a proper, vetted constitutionalist. To President Bush's credit, he found Judge Samuel Alito, a brilliant strict constitutionalist who would have made Chief Justice Rehnquist proud. Democrats once again did their devil best to smear and destroy Alito, but Republicans held their ground and got him confirmed. On the high court, Alito soon made his mark in alliance with fellow Justices Clarence Thomas and Antonin Scalia as a rock solid constitutionalist.

LITIGIOUS CONSTITUTIONALIST

By the time Donald Trump descended his glass escalator into the wasteland that was the American political scene, it is safe to say that I had become a fairly radicalized Supreme Court voter. I had seen up close and firsthand what conservative voters across the country knew instinctively: the battle for the soul of our country was being fought in the federal courts, far from the reaches of electoral politics.

It was not the battlefield of our choosing. It was the battlefield chosen by Ted Kennedy and his leftist army.

For conservatives, the idea of a political fight over the courts is the opposite of what the courts are supposed to be about. Judges are supposed to be impartial, fiercely nonpartisan protectors of our individual constitutional liberties. They do not make law. They do not execute laws. They stand as a safeguard to ensure that governments, the legislature, and the executive branch never trample on our freedoms.

In the months after Trump announced his campaign for presidency, some of my oldest friends in Washington recited the same unfounded refrain over and over again about Trump.

"Lawless! A tyrant! Trump will shred the Constitution!"

This always amused me, especially after eight years of Barack Obama, whose tenure was dominated by lawlessness.

President Obama refused to enforce basic federal laws, such as the Defense of Marriage Act. After years of correctly saying he did not have the constitutional authority to protect illegal aliens from prosecution and deportation, he summarily did just that with the Deferred Action for Childhood Arrivals and Deferred Action for Parents of Americans programs. In other cases, such as with Obamacare, President Obama simply used administrative maneuvering to rewrite the law passed by Congress whenever it suited him. And let's not forget Obama's top law enforcement officer in the land, Attorney General Eric

Holder, became the first cabinet official in U.S. history to be held in contempt of Congress over his refusal to hand over documents relating to the Department of Justice's "Fast and Furious" international gun smuggling operation.

All this hysterical pearl-clutching about Trump's supposed disdain for the Constitution rang a little hollow to me.

Anyway, I argued back, have you ever looked at all the people Donald Trump has sued over the decades he worked as a successful real estate mogul, reality star, and celebrity? I mean, the guy sued everyone from Merv Griffin to a Miss America contestant for reasons ranging from casino dealings to Trump branding issues.

How could a guy who has launched as many lawsuits as Trump has over the course of his career not have at least some regard for the Constitution? If elected, I told these people, Trump would be the most litigiously aggressive president in American history! How could such a guy not want to protect the Constitution? Among the most blindly afflicted by Trump Derangement Syndrome, this argument carried little sway.

I will admit, it was not an ironclad argument. But then again, nothing is ironclad in politics. Especially when it comes to federal judges.

Just ask Ronald Reagan, George H. W. Bush, and George W. Bush. Reagan fared better than the others. But the Bushes were the Forrest Gumps of the federal judiciary. For them, judicial nominations were like a box of chocolates. You just never knew what you were gonna get.

One of my dearest friends who lost her mind over Donald Trump once concluded a heated tirade by saying: "You just watch! It is going to be so funny when this madman becomes president and nominates his sister to the Supreme Court. And it will be all your fault."

I would be lying if I said that didn't send shivers through me.

While I recognized in Trump a deeply careful listener with unmatched political instincts, what really did I know about his judicial philosophy? Did he know the difference between a Ruth Bader Ginsburg, a David Souter, and a William Rehnquist? The things that made him such a smart politician—transactionally principled, pragmatically goal oriented, and ill-tempered when necessary—were not exactly the ingredients of a good judicial philosophy. Still, something deep down gave me faith that while Trump himself would not make a very good Supreme Court justice, he had the wisdom, smarts, and patience to figure out who would.

Then came February 13, 2016. It was a Saturday and we were at my grandmother's farm down in Orange County, Virginia, outside the small hamlet of Rapidan. It was a sunny winter day and we had spent the short daylight hours marching through the woods with the children and the dogs, looking for fresh deer antler sheds and taking in the glorious sights of the distant Blue Ridge Mountains.

The dining room was set for an early dinner and we were about to sit down when I remembered that I had not looked at my phone since the morning. I needed to check in just to make sure Washington had not burned to the ground or Florida had not been invaded by ISIS. The news could not possibly have been a swifter blow to the gut.

Supreme Court justice Antonin Scalia was dead.

After I had gathered my wits, my family assembled around the table. Like millions of Americans that evening, we said the blessing, making a special point to remember Justice Scalia's family.

During dinner, the children were most interested in hearing about Scalia. Who was he? Why was he important? What did he do on the Supreme Court? How did he die? How old was he?

If you cover politics for a living, yet you believe that politics should make up but a tiny fraction of a family's life, moments like these can be difficult to strike a balance. You look for that balance between understanding the true and real gravity of a political threat from actors inside the federal government and confidence that this extraordinary system of checks and balances the Founders devised for us can withstand any such bad actors.

In seeking that balance, this was one of those cases where I failed miserably.

By the time I finished answering all of their questions and describing the monumental importance of Justice Scalia and just how much of a patriot the great man was, I looked up from my meal. The children had all stopped eating. Utensils still on their plates, hands in their laps, they stared at me.

We were sitting just about twenty miles as the crow flies from James Madison's Montpelier, where each of the children had spent summers attending "mud camp." We were at the place where their great-grandmother and great-grandfather had raised a family running a cattle farm. For the children, it was a land where they learned to shoot guns, had Bible study in the yard with their grandmother, and celebrated every fruit of American freedom under the sun.

I don't remember what I told them about Justice Scalia and his importance to preserving freedom and a way of life, but it must have been a pretty scalding oration. They sat staring at me with wide eyes, bulging near tears. They wanted to know what would happen next.

And who would replace Justice Scalia.

It was one of those singular moments in your life as a parent when you have no answer. You are completely helpless. All you can do is step off a receding ledge of solid hope onto a nearly invisible cloud of faith. And not because you are a particularly faithful person or some kind of wise Christian. But because you have no other choice.

Looking back on that moment today and remembering the hopelessness I felt over the loss of Justice Antonin Scalia, I marvel at how it all worked out. Truly, it is one of those times where you cannot help but think that the good Lord really does have a special place in His heart for the United States.

It was sometime later that Donald Trump instructed the respected constitutionalist Leonard Leo of the Federalist Society to help craft a list of carefully vetted federal judges from which he would choose any Supreme Court nominees. It turned out to be a brilliant ploy that calmed the concerns of millions of conservative voters worried about Donald Trump's own lack of a record when it came to picking federal judges.

The lion's share of credit goes to Trump himself, but also important was not only Leonard Leo's contribution but also Senate Majority Leader Mitch McConnell, who made the bold gamble shortly after Justice Scalia died that he would keep the vacancy open until a new president was elected to succeed Obama, who was in his final year of office. Of course, most observers figured that would be Hillary Clinton. But to conservative constitutionalist voters around the country, nothing inspires them to the polls more than a chance to inject sanity into the federal courts, especially the Supreme Court. It would prove to be one of the biggest issues that got Trump elected.

President Trump has remained faithful to his promise to work from the list of carefully vetted federal jurists. Even the most die-hard Never Trumper Republicans cannot help but admit that this has been an unalloyed victory for conservatives. Supreme Court justice Neil Gorsuch brings to the bench a fidelity to the Constitution that would make Justice Scalia proud. And few constitutionalists have spent more years than Justice Brett Kavanaugh slogging away in the bowels of constitutional arguments in Washington.

If you have any doubt about how effective Gorsuch and Kavanaugh will be, just look at the toxic, vitriolic smear campaign Democrats waged against Kavanaugh. It was as dishonest as it was unfair and desperate, a perfect reflection of just how much these leftist Democrats see at stake over the Supreme Court.

At the lowest moment of the Kavanaugh hearings—after the man had been slimed with the most scurrilous and unhinged accusations imaginable—President Trump publicly defended his nominee. He said he would withdraw the nomination if he thought any of the accusations were remotely true. He did not. When all the smoke and cannon fire finally cleared, President Trump was still standing behind his nominee. It was a display of political fortitude never before seen in these judicial wars.

Finally, Ted Kennedy and his cabal of lawless miscreants had met their match, in President Donald Trump.

★CHAPTER SIX★

HILLARY THE WARMONGER

I consider myself about as worldly and well traveled as the next guy. I have been all over Europe, banged up more than my share of rental cars in countries where they drive on the wrong side of the road.

I went behind the Iron Curtain and have been to the God-forsaken Middle East more than once. As a kid I spent a summer working in a hospital in the remote jungles of Africa. I survived a pretty nasty strain of malaria.

I have even been to Canada. Though I have never felt the tug to spend much time in Mexico, I buy all of my fireworks at South of the Border (in South Carolina) and love all those little border towns in Texas and New Mexico and Arizona.

I draw the line at California.

But, like the vast majority of Americans, I would not present myself as any particular foreign policy expert. It really is one of the luxuries of having almost an entire continent to ourselves.

If good fences make good neighbors, vast oceans make the best neighbors. Tall walls also make good neighbors.

President Trump visits graves of U.S. veterans in France (Saul Loeb)

Quick aside: Why is it that when all the rich white celebrities in America threatened to leave the country if Donald Trump won the election, they threatened to move to Canada?

Why Canada? Why do they want to go to the whitest country in the hemisphere? What is wrong with Honduras or Venezuela? Or even Mexico? It's right next door, too?

My second—and far more important question—is why don't these rich white celebrities ever keep their grand promises? We would all be so much happier and America would be so much better off if they would actually pony up on all their big talk and move to another country. Talk about Making America Great Again!

All of this is by way of saying that I am not an entirely unworldly person. And, while I have lived much of my adult life in a couple of fairly cosmopolitan cities—Detroit and Washington, D.C.—I do not suffer from any kind of profound anxiety about being an American. In fact, I am incredibly proud of being an American. Always have been. Always will be.

The vast majority of people I have lived and worked around in the big city—particularly your nation's capital—are more than just a hint embarrassed about being American. Deep down, they wish to be French or Vietnamese or Italian. At the very least, they would like to possess a sort of international personal stature. Now, these are good people. They love their children and raise them with discipline. They work hard and pursue honesty. But they really do consider themselves citizens of the world, rather than Americans. This is particularly true among reporters—even more particularly so among political reporters in Washington, D.C.

For these people, there is no greater plum assignment than to be sent to Moscow to report for several years. Or Buenos

Aires. They jump at any chance to go abroad, which I certainly understand. I share that sense of adventure. It is why I spent six years in Detroit.

But these people, they go abroad, they cover stories unique to whatever region of the world they went to, and then they come home and never stop talking about it. It's as if, somehow, the plummeting exchange rate on the value of Persian rugs between Russia and Iran is vitally important to the average guy walking down the street in some town in America. Now, I like Oriental rugs as much as the next guy, but I can tell you that it is not a pressing matter to your average reader here in America.

These internationalist Americans come back from their travels thoroughly infected with the idea that they—and therefore all of their fellow Americans—should give a rip about international rug prices in Iran and Russia. When they find out people don't want to listen to them going on and on about the injustice or this or that in Persia or wherever, they reach the disastrously wrong conclusion that the oblivious Americans are stupid.

No, actually. They are very smart. They have their priorities straight. Top ten include things like their family, their neighbors, their job, their church, their car, and so on. Along about 10,495th on their list of priorities is—quite wisely—the price of rugs in Iran.

Most of them—understandably—are far more concerned about the price of gasoline at the nearest service station. Oddly, the most worldly Americans may be farmers who deal with international pricing and world market demands more than most major industries. A farmer, however, doesn't care about the price of a rug. He is most concerned about what he is going to get this year for his crop of soybeans or corn or wheat.

Let's take something a little less ridiculous than the price of Persian rugs on the global market. Let's consider the condition of people living in a hellhole under a vicious dictator in a faraway place like Syria. Or Libya. Places someone less politically attuned might call "sh*tholes."

In no way do I mean to belittle the plight of the good men, women, and children who must live in these horrid places. As an American, I believe our right to govern ourselves comes directly from God. No king, government, or dictator has the right to interfere with that blessing from God. But that does not mean that all the problems of the world belong to me. Or my neighbors here in America. Or my children or my cousins. Or my country.

There are really sad things going on all over this mean, rotten world. But I am not responsible for them. And just because we are the freest, richest, most powerful country on the planet does not in any way mean that we are somehow suddenly responsible for all of the ills of the world.

If you purchased a book written by me, you probably already understand this. Your list of global priorities are fairly well—and wisely—settled. The incalculable miseries of some forgotten third-world barbaric state are nowhere near as important as your responsibility to make car pool on time for your children and the three other kids you pick up for school three times a week.

But these internationalist Americans view it differently. Radically differently. The squalid problems of some miserable spit of desert more than six thousand miles away is bizarrely important to an alarming number of people in this country. And, most terrifyingly, an alarming number of those people hold powerful positions here in America, particularly in the professions of the media and politics. And it is not necessarily a partisan thing.

Powerful luminaries from both parties have feasted at the banquet table of America's military-industrial complex for decades. Usually the only people who are not represented at that feast are the ones who wind up paying the most grievous price for that international adventurism.

Even to this day, reasonable people in America can debate whether or not we should have allowed ourselves to get dragged into World War II. After all, we paid an enormous price during that conflict in terms of blood and treasure. Those costs in terms of treasure only grew higher with the rebuilding of Europe and Japan. And, for the most part, the fighting was almost entirely over lands far, far away from the United States.

Without a doubt, it was a shining moment of sterling heroism for so many Americans fighting on the front lines of Europe and the Pacific. To this day the sacrifices those men and women made are hard to entirely comprehend.

To be sure, it was, in fact, a "world war" in every literal sense. Practically no corner of the globe was not consumed by the conflagration. Even living on a massive continent protected by broad seas did not entirely protect America from the fierce winds of that war. Beyond the savage fighting, the political winds, too, profoundly affected our tidy island home. A Europe controlled by Adolf Hitler or Joseph Stalin would have been intolerable and eventually would have dragged us into a war of survival. The Far East, controlled by the lunatic emperor of Japan, was not far enough away, as obviously evidenced by the bombing of our air and naval bases at Pearl Harbor.

No matter how much of an ardent anti-interventionist you may be, we can all agree that the United States spectacularly achieved our goals in that war. Part of the reason for our success was how clearly defined the mission was—unlike our muddled efforts in places like Vietnam. We responded to Japan's sneak attack with a ferocity that has remained a warning to vicious despots the world over during the more than seventy years since we dropped atomic bombs on Hiroshima and Nagasaki. We eliminated Hitler's rapacious German army and freed Jews from his concentration camps. Finally, we struck a cool peace with expansionist Russia that at least put off the inevitable long enough to recover from the war.

By the time all the dust settled from World War II, the American economy was booming, the Soviets were starving, the Jews had a homeland, and Germany and Japan were being rebuilt into responsible industrial countries. In time, Germany and Japan would enjoy the second- and third-largest economies on the planet, just behind the United States of America. Tiny little Israel's economy would be among the top twenty in the world.

Whatever you think about getting into World War II, it is pretty hard to argue with the success of it. Obviously, it came at an enormous sacrifice both in terms of financial cost to the United States and in terms of men and women who sacrificed their lives or forever paid the price of injury and horror, particularly during fighting in the Pacific.

There was another cost of World War II that is rarely discussed. But it is a heavy one that many Americans have paid dearly in the decades since. Ironically, it stems from the unalloyed success of World War II.

Sure, people came home from that war. They kissed girls, got married, and started families. They bought homes and built tidy neighborhoods. They enjoyed a postwar economic boom that lifted unprecedented numbers of Americans into a new, burgeoning "middle class." It was a sudden economic boom rarely seen on such a scale in human history. Regular Americans rightly enjoyed every fruit of their nation's joyous success.

Outside of those growing neighborhoods with nice yards and new cars, powerful people in places like Washington, D.C., were eyeing other fruits of that time. The dizzying success of World War II demonstrated the unrivaled global power that was the United States. To those early swamp creatures, it also revealed that the levers of power in the American government could be used to turn the United States into a policeman of the world.

President Dwight Eisenhower, our last general-turned-president, was most prescient in warning against allowing the military-industrial complex to take root in Washington. Sadly, leaders of both parties ultimately ignored that stark warning.

Always for the most understandable and noble reasons, American leaders have been drawn into foreign conflicts: Settling foreign aggression abroad. Containing communism. Keeping global adversaries in check.

Barely back from war in Europe and Japan under President Franklin Roosevelt, Democrat presidents Harry Truman, John F. Kennedy, and Lyndon B. Johnson got us thoroughly mired in wars in Southeast Asia. President Trump is still dealing with the broken pieces left behind in a now-nuclear Korean Peninsula.

Our entanglement in the Vietnam War was even more costly in terms of blood, treasure, and the American psyche. Vietnam was a perfect example of the globalist geniuses in Washington thinking they were smart enough to fix some far-flung part of the world. And the boys who paid the heaviest price for that intervention often were not the sons of the people making those decisions.

Casualties mounted against an obstinate enemy and with little hope in sight. For all his failings, President Richard Nixon at least understood the need to disentangle from an enemy far, far away who was not going anywhere. The original purpose for getting involved may have remained a noble one. But Nixon was smart enough to ask whether it was worth the ongoing price. Which, of course, it wasn't.

The vast and extensive lies that generals and politicians in Washington wove to maintain the facade of progress in Vietnam only further damaged America's trust in government. It caused many of America's most patriotic families—the very same families whose loved ones fought so bravely in World War II—to wonder about the price they were paying and whether their government could even be trusted.

In many ways, the families who paid the dearest price during Vietnam would eventually become the "forgotten" men and women who decades later would rush into the embrace of the brash New York real estate magnate Donald Trump.

One of the biggest problems about staying out of foreign wars is that American voters tend to rally around a president in any war. This is because Americans are decent people who assume their leaders are doing their homework as diligently as Americans take care of their own families and businesses. If our leader says there's a need and a cause worth fighting for, then Americans are there to answer the call.

In a perfect world, never would a president get us into a war or launch air strikes in order to distract attention away from some brewing sex scandal back home. President Clinton's timing back in 1998 was purely coincidental, he insisted. The airstrikes just happened to have come the day after House Republicans delivered impeachment charges against Clinton.

But, as you may recall, the Iraqi air strikes were supposedly about getting Saddam Hussein's regime to cooperate with United Nations weapons inspectors—not about distracting from the politics at home. Only a rank skeptic would have any doubts about this.

It's that trust in leaders during wartime that leads to the added political benefit of a boost in poll numbers. The highest approval rating Gallup had ever registered was for President George H. W. Bush after he invaded Iraq in retaliation for Iraq's invasion of Kuwait, until his son—President George W. Bush—topped that record in the aftermath of the September 11, 2001, terrorist attacks.

Since politicians cannot contain themselves around the mesmerizing elixir known as poll numbers, they tend to get really excited around military hardware and all manner of international interventionism. With America positioned as the world's policeman there's always some conflict somewhere that leaders can justify getting involved in.

The only problem is that these spikes in poll numbers around military actions are more like sugar highs—they don't last.

Needless to say, about a year after his skyrocketing poll numbers, George H. W. Bush got booted out of the White House. His son also saw a serious drop in the polls as the aftermath of 9/11 led to another Iraqi invasion as well as a war in Afghanistan. Both engagements have lingered for decades beyond what was originally promised. America had once again become involved in the tricky business of nation building in a faraway land.

None of this is to say that either Bush threw down the gauntlet to protect the sacred sovereignty of Kuwait or avenge those lost on 9/11 just to goose poll numbers. But the added political boost is always dangerous, especially when a president is surrounded by youthful advisers whose job it is to look to the next campaign. As an adviser to the president, a political operative can't help but think that way and advise his client, in this case the president, as such.

Certainly, I do not believe President George W. Bush got us into the Iraq War for any kind of underhanded political purposes or for any ulterior motives, for that matter. The tangible bloodlust in the aftermath of 9/11 was so potent that action was needed. The country had witnessed three thousand of its fellow citizens suffer an unimaginable end only because they were Americans. We saw two of our most prominent symbols of America in ashes because they represented a way of life deemed unacceptable to another group of people. We heard the heroic stories of those who crash-landed their passenger plane in a field in Pennsylvania, likely saving hundreds more in the nation's capital.

Indeed, one of the things I have always admired about President Bush and Vice President Dick Cheney is that I have never doubted that they got us into the Iraq War for anything other than their stated reasons. There was an opportunity not just to show the world that any attack on America was unacceptable, but also to try to prevent another event like that from happening again. They believed that Saddam Hussein and despot thugs like him anywhere around the world posed a grave danger to peace and security in the United States. If the choice was between intervention and prevention or hoping and waiting, then the decision was simple.

The conspiracy theory suggesting that oil was at the heart of the decision just doesn't hold up. Like it or not, the Middle East is a player on the world stage because of its oil reserves. Thus those countries cannot simply be dismissed or ignored— even though their hold over the world has shifted somewhat in modern times.

But the idea that we would launch a costly war to depose a vicious dictator more than six thousand miles away, only to create a vacuum that would be filled by the next most vicious force in the area, over oil is ridiculous. Moreover, time has shown that America's dependence on foreign oil was not permanent. In 2018, America ended its dependence on foreign oil and became a net exporter for the first time in seventy-five years. Also, if the war in Iraq was about oil, wouldn't the better strategy have been to invade Saudi Arabia, which produces far more oil than Iraq? The theory of oil as the heart of the issue in the Iraq War just doesn't hold up.

The larger problem with the war is that we believed that our closely held principles of life, liberty, and the pursuit of happiness would be universally shared. Did we really think that after decades of merciless subjugation by the most bloodthirsty despots, the people of Iraq would rise up and joyously fall into line under a peaceful form of democracy? The lives lost and money spent over there showed us that no amount of action or resources can put that desire in the hearts of people. The people have to have that fire for freedom themselves. It's that fire that inspired our troops to go there in the first place and it's what makes us want to pursue these global conflicts.

But there are sacrifices to these overseas efforts. Think of what more than $5 trillion might have done here at home:

the schools it could have built, the job programs it could have
created, and the health care it could have provided for those
coming home from these military campaigns.

Most unthinkable are the lives sacrificed and heroes who
came back home utterly broken. Post-traumatic stress disorder
has only recently become a topic of conversation, but many
suffered silently after serving honorably overseas. A 2018 report
from the Department of Veterans Affairs showed the suicide
rate among young veterans ages 18–34 increased by more than
10 percent between 2015 and 2016 and the suicide rate among
veterans overall is 1.5 times higher than for those who've never
served. Others come home with missing limbs or severe head
trauma that will stay with them for the rest of their lives.

These sacrifices are among the easiest to forget in
Washington, where the decisions are made by politicians.
The generational gap between those who served in World
War II and remember the sacrifices of war versus those who
avoided the draft in Vietnam is evidenced by the leadership
in Washington. It's easier to disregard the sacrifices of war
if you've never served. These considerations may change as
more of those veterans from Iraq and Afghanistan run for
office and are part of the conversation when considering the
next invasion.

To be sure, President Bush never relented in his optimism
that the war in Iraq was justified and wise. His determination
to win that war never flagged. And his devotion to the men
and women he sent to carry out his orders in that foreign land
never wavered. His commitment to them has remained strong
even after leaving office. And his rare times in the spotlight
postpresidency are almost always to promote a veterans'
cause.

The same cannot be said about many politicians down Pennsylvania Avenue in the U.S. Capitol, where lasting positions on the war depend on which way the latest wind is blowing. In the beginning, back in 2002, there was strong unity by politicians in favor of going to war. The United States Senate voted 77–23 in favor of war, with 29 Democrats joining Republicans. In the House, the vote was 297–133, with 82 Democrats joining in.

But the amazing and enraging thing is not how bipartisan the vote was in favor of war; it is how many of those politicians who voted in favor of the war would later declare they had made a mistake. Their commitment went no further than hitting a button to vote, while America's precious youth were dying in a foreign cesspool. All these elected "leaders" cared about was political gain.

Just listen to the words of two of the biggest political warriors who later deserted the men and women they had sent out onto the battlefield.

"We are in possession of what I think to be compelling evidence that Saddam Hussein has, and has had for a number of years, a developing capacity for the production and storage of weapons of mass destruction," declared John Kerry, the insufferable Democrat from Massachusetts. "Without question, we need to disarm Saddam Hussein," Kerry labored on. "He is a brutal, murderous dictator, leading an oppressive regime."

Not to be outdone, then-senator John Edwards went even further: "I think Iraq is the most serious and important threat to our country and I think Iraq and Saddam Hussein present the most serious and imminent threat." Edwards, a personal injury lawyer from North Carolina, was so bloodthirsty for war that he even cosponsored an earlier version of the Iraq War resolution, though his bill never reached the floor.

Within two years, Kerry and Edwards both turned against the war and busied themselves running a presidential campaign against President Bush. The main issue in that campaign was the war in Iraq, the war that both men had voted for.

Both Kerry and Edwards will go down in history as the political buffoons they are. If cemeteries were just and true, John Kerry's tombstone would be a giant granite pretzel. His epitaph would read: "I actually did vote for the $87 billion before I voted against it." That famous flip-flop would be in reference to the bill he voted for to keep funding the war in Iraq that he had voted in favor of but then turned against.

And then later voted not to fund. After voting to fund.

If there had not been so many lives of people so much worthier than John Kerry or John Edwards on the line, it would have all been funny. But young men and women were dying. They were coming home horribly maimed. There was nothing funny about any of it.

John Kerry's insufferable self-regard was legendary among the press in 2004, even if it rarely leaked into most of the coverage of his campaign. Reporters made little secret of their certainty that there was no way President Bush could win re-election.

I was pool reporter on the eve of the Democrat Convention in Boston that year when Kerry went to Fenway Park to throw out the ceremonial first pitch in a game against their arch rival Yankees. There to catch Kerry's pitch was a soldier, back from Iraq, who supported Kerry for president.

I described the mixture of boos and applause Kerry

received as he walked out onto the field towards the pitcher's mound. He took his position in the grass so that he could make a little league throw to the soldier squatting behind home plate.

"Kerry then gave a gangly, long-armed windup about two feet into the green grass from the mound," I wrote in my pool report. "It was a soft pitch that stayed aloft until hitting the dirt between the legs and under the soldier."

In other words, despite the little league set-up, Kerry still could not get the ball across the plate. Of course, I had to ask him about that.

Astonishingly, his immediate response was to blame the soldier.

"I held back," Kerry replied. "He was very nervous. I tried to lob it gently."

So, it wasn't enough to vote for a war to send this guy to Iraq, then to run a presidential campaign against the war you voted for? John Kerry also had to call the soldier some kind of Nervous Nelly when he himself could not throw a little league baseball across home plate.

Even more enraging was the later discovery of just how little homework many of these senators did before voting for the war—far and away the most serious decision any politician can ever make. When you are sending young people to die in war, doing a little research isn't too much to ask.

A few years later, a 2007 report by *The Hill* newspaper revealed that only "a handful of senators outside the Intelligence Committee say they read the full 92-page National Intelligence Estimate on Iraq's ability to attack the U.S. before voting to go to war."

John Kerry, who did not read the complete assessment, was unrepentant: "I read the summary, but I didn't read the full report because I got it from them straight," referring to personal briefings he had with senior Bush administration officials.

John Edwards told a town hall gathering that, in fact, he had read the whole report. That was not true. But it was in the run-up to yet another presidential election so, you know, whatever. Say what you need to say to get what you need to get regardless of the consequences to anyone else.

When confronted with Edwards's false statement, his campaign later acknowledged that Edwards had not, in fact, read the report.

To be fair, few people on either side of the aisle felt any responsibility to read the full intelligence report. After all, it was a whole ninety-two pages long.

"A lot of people on both sides of the aisle are getting whacked around with this," lamented one Republican who voted for the war. "You have to understand that the briefings are so thorough that it's common for members not to read entire reports."

Complained a Democrat who also voted for the war: "Well, I don't think anybody read the entire report. Everybody gets summaries of it."

As wrong as John Edwards may have been to vote for the war in Iraq, he never displayed an ounce of humility about it. "I was wrong to vote for this war," he said during a debate running up to the 2008 election. "Unfortunately, I'll have to live with that forever and a lesson I learned from it is to put more faith in my own judgment."

His own judgment!

One of my very first assignments when I arrived in Washington in 2001 was to cover John Edwards, then a rising new Democrat heartthrob serving a term as a North Carolina senator. His only claim to fame was that he had been passed over as Al Gore's running mate in the 2000 campaign. I covered him for the *Charlotte Observer* and fairly soon figured out what a slickster he was and his penchant for playing fast and loose with facts—and, as it turned out, with other people's lives.

His wife, Elizabeth, was another matter. She could be blisteringly honest and often hilarious. I spent a good deal of time with her in the run-up to the 2004 election.

Later, after she had battled and battled cancer, John Edwards was exposed for his lecherous ways. Most famously, of course, he got caught by the *National Enquirer* for fathering a child with a videographer who was following his campaign.

As all of those revelations tumbled out into the public, I was haunted by something Elizabeth told me sometime after *People* magazine named her husband the "sexiest" politician.

"Anybody who knows anything about John knows that he's lived his life in a personal way considerably different than how President Clinton did," she told me. Her friends, she said, would gush about him and tell her she had landed "one of the good ones."

In his political decision to abandon the brave youngsters he had voted to send to war, he was right in line with the way he ultimately trashed his devoted wife. The only silver lining is that was about the last we ever heard from John Edwards.

Unfortunately, the same cannot be said about John Kerry.

One of the great forgotten ironies about President Bush's successful reelection in 2004 was just how much that election was a referendum on the war in Iraq. That is kind of funny when you consider that everybody on both sides of the ticket agreed to go to war in Iraq in the first place.

It was just that the Democrats—mainly presidential candidates John Kerry and John Edwards—had abandoned the war just as soon as it was politically expedient for them to do so.

Even more curious about that whole election is that it wasn't just the general election that became all about the war. The Democrat primary was also all about the war. Remember Howard Dean? And his crazed orange-hatted "Deaniacs"? The scream?

The former governor was the first major candidate to really capitalize on the growing regret inside the Democrat Party that so many party leaders had voted America into war in Iraq.

Just about every Democrat surveying the cornfields of Iowa that year had actually supported the invasion. Yet Howard Dean's antiwar ravings were manna to starved voters. So while some of those boys who grew up in the cornfields were fighting in a desert more than six thousand miles away, the men who sent them there were calculating the political benefit of saying it was all a mistake.

The crazy scream after Dean faltered in Iowa was like dynamite unleashing avalanches of snow. Calculations fed upon calculations and Democrats who loved Howard Dean and his antiwar credentials instead lined up behind John Kerry, who voted for the war but was now campaigning against it. Democrats were unashamed of straddling the line of supporting the war when it was popular but agreeing it was a mistake when national sentiment changed.

"Dated Dean, Married Kerry," was the bumper sticker back then. And then Kerry picked Edwards and the ticket sounded like some sorority cheerleading duo, not to insult cheerleaders. The bet was misplaced, however, and the duo found that walking the line between war and peace was a lot harder than expected.

Four years later, Democrats were not about to make the same mistake again. Cashiered were all the fakers, especially the ones who had voted in favor of the war. John Kerry was gone. Edwards's goose was cooked. In 2008, Hillary Clinton made a valiant effort that would have exhausted Cujo, but even she eventually surrendered. Instead of going with an antiwar faker who had voted for the war, Democrats at least chose in Tim Kaine an antiwar faker who at least had not actually voted for the Iraq War.

OBAMA THE WAR MONGER

The whole reason America suffered eight years of President Barack Obama was the Iraq War and the 111 Democrats in Congress who voted to invade Saddam Hussein's thugocracy in the aftermath of 9/11.

In the first place, it is entirely probable that if Democrats had fielded a decent candidate in 2004 who had not voted for the war, they could have won the general election. John Kerry was a blowhard embarrassment from the start and even Democrats could not take him seriously.

Four years later, Democrats were hardened in pursuit of a nominee who had not voted for the war. For all the talk in D.C. and elite political party circles about how Hillary Clinton was a shoo-in, regular Democrat voters from California to Iowa to New York and across the country were clearly hungry for a candidate who could freely prosecute an argument against the war without any reservation.

Incredibly they ended up with Hillary Clinton as that nominee. As much time and energy as she spent blaming her loss on her gender, it was actually all about her vote for the Iraq War. That and the fact that she always seemed to be lying and after a lifetime in the political spotlight, she remained terribly unlikable (or, as Obama would observe about her, "likable enough").

It really did not matter to Democrats that the only reason for Barack Obama's sterling record on the war is that he simply never faced a vote on the war during his short tenure in the United States Senate.

In the Illinois state legislature, Obama was famous for voting "present" to avoid casting ticklish or uncomfortable votes. Had he been in the U.S. Senate in 2002, he could not have gotten away with avoiding a vote on the war. His seatmate, Senator Dick Durbin, confidently voted against the war so perhaps it would have been an easy call for Obama.

To be fair, Obama was always consistent in saying he would have voted against the war if he had been given a chance. Obviously, his voters took him on his word about that. But the amazing thing is the way that Obama entirely abandoned those antiwar voters and the entire platform that got him elected just as soon as he got into the White House.

Even though the Obama campaign kicked me off his campaign plane over a column I wrote—ironically enough, about the Iraq War—I admired the positive, unifying, hopeful, and even nonpartisan campaign that he ran in 2008. "There is not a black America and a white America and Latino America and Asian America—there's the United States of America," he told us during the 2004 Democrat convention.

Ha! If only he had governed that way.

Same with all his promises about war.

The first clue that President Obama had no intention of keeping his antiwar promises came before he even got into the

White House, when word leaked that he was sneaking around with his great pro-war nemesis, Hillary Clinton herself.

He wanted to put her in charge of diplomacy around the world.

Stop and think about it. Hillary Clinton had lost the Democrat nomination because she voted for the Iraq war. The whole party had lost the previous election because they picked a pro-war nominee to head their ticket. And here was President Obama picking Hillary Clinton to be secretary of state, where she would be in charge of Obama's supposedly antiwar policy agenda around the globe.

This would be no different than President Trump getting elected on promises to disengage from military entanglements around the world and then picking former vice president Dick Cheney to be his secretary of state. Rightly, Trump supporters would have gone bananas.

Making further mockery of his antiwar campaign pledges, President Obama later picked pro–Iraq War flip-flopper John Kerry to replace Hillary Clinton after she got done delivering so much world peace as secretary of state. For her tenure waging peace around the world, Clinton will be best remembered for the U.S. drone attack that led to the killing of ousted strongman Muammar Gaddafi after he had surrendered Libya's weapons of mass destruction to previous president George W. Bush.

"We came, we saw, he died," Clinton joked in 2011, laughing.

Peace.

Her tenure of peace will also forever be remembered by the subsequent attack on the U.S. consulate in Benghazi, Libya, a year later in which four Americans were killed. In typical Clintonian fashion, she immediately lied about the attack, refusing to acknowledge that it was a coordinated attack planned for the anniversary of 9/11. Instead, she falsely blamed an anti-Muslim Internet video for the attack. Clinton's promotion of the video caused the video to go viral around the world. That in turn sparked outrage among Muslims around the world in response to the video. In the aftermath, dozens of people were killed in riots around the world. Hundreds more were injured.

Peace.

None of this is to say that President Obama was going to be held to account for his desertion of antiwar voters. At least not from the globalist elites around the world who seem to really love spending your money and sending your boys into war zones.

In 2009, not even a year into office, much of the world was shocked when President Obama was awarded the Nobel Peace Prize. In announcing it, the Nobel Committee cited Obama's "extraordinary efforts to strengthen international diplomacy and cooperation between peoples."

For a mere mortal, this would have been rather awkward. Obama had not ended the war in Iraq as promised and he had not ended the war in Afghanistan. Several years later, according to the BBC, Geir Lundestad, who was secretary of the Nobel Committee when Obama's award was given, expressed regret over the decision. Stating that the committee had hoped the award would strengthen Obama's resolve, it had not done so. Stated Secretary Lundestad: "Even many of Obama's supporters believed that the prize was a mistake." In fact, even as he was accepting the Nobel Peace Prize, Obama was planning a massive troop surge in Afghanistan from roughly 25,000 troops when he came into office to 100,000 U.S. troops.

Before Obama's terms were over, he would also expand U.S. engagements around the world. In addition to Afghanistan, Iraq, and Libya, the U.S. would launch air strikes into Syria, Yemen, Somalia, and Pakistan, all under Obama's orders. When he left office, Obama was the only two-term president in history to oversee eight years of war.

Good thing he won his Nobel Peace Prize so early in his presidency.

In the 2016 campaign, Donald Trump's foreign policy platform was as simple as it was popular: Maintain a mighty military that can destroy anything on earth, enforce strong borders around our homeland, and stay out of unnecessary foreign entanglements as much as possible. Don't get mired in foreign conflicts where U.S. interests are not at risk and where the objective is not clearly defined.

Throughout American history, this has always been the most popular foreign policy platform. Such a position would have clearly spared us involvement in Vietnam and Korea and plenty of other painful adventures. It probably would have allowed for our involvement in World War II. Same with Afghanistan after 9/11.

The Iraq War remains an open question, though not in Donald Trump's mind. "Such a waste of money," Trump told me. "What? We spend three, four, five trillion dollars? That's 'trillion' with a *t*!"

Nothing animates Donald Trump like throwing money away. In his mind, it is not just stupid, it is actually immoral. "And what do we get out of it? Nothing. We didn't even get any oil out of it. Such a waste!"

Trump's honesty is so refreshing here. Even supporters of the war in the so-called neocon wing of the Republican

Party were aghast at the accusation that President Bush would launch a war in the Middle East over oil. That would be so low and grubby and dirty. But to President Trump, fighting for oil is at the very least a winning proposition. If you are going to fight a war to fix somebody else's country, you might as well get compensated for it.

That is, after all, a pretty American way of looking at it.

Still, from the start Trump was not buying into the Iraq War.

In February 2016, Trump turned his sights on the South Carolina primary. He had just won a blowout victory in New Hampshire. Now, Trump might be cheap when it comes to spending money on unnecessary wars, but that doesn't mean he doesn't believe in spending big on things that matter. He views political capital the same way.

Sitting in his suite in Trump International in Las Vegas during an interview, I wondered whether Trump liked to gamble. There is not a casino in his hotel there.

For some reason, he did not seem to want to answer my question. I asked him every way I could think of and he kept evading my question.

Finally, he threw open his hands, cocked his head, and flashed that gangster smile he's got. "Hey, look," he said, almost defensively, "my whole life is a gamble."

Indeed. I could only laugh.

And in South Carolina, Trump aimed to prove that point after building plenty of capital with his big New Hampshire victory. South Carolina is one of the most conservative states in the country. It has a huge military presence. You will not find a greater display of patriotism on the campaign trail than in South Carolina.

Also, South Carolina loves George W. Bush. That is where the insurgent John McCain's primary campaign against Bush died in 2000. Bush would go on to beat Al Gore there by 15 points in 2000 and trounce John Kerry there by 17 points in 2004. The state was a make-or-break race for Bush's little brother, Jeb Bush, who had once been considered the 2016 front-runner.

So South Carolina is by no means some kind of hotbed of antiwar hippies. If anything, quite the opposite.

But Trump went into South Carolina with a full attack on George W. Bush and eviscerated the argument for the Iraq War. Talk about a gamble. He called the Iraq War a mistake and said it did nothing to keep America safe. He said it was a waste of money and accused the Bush administration of lying about weapons of mass destruction.

Voters were stunned by the harshness of Trump's assault on the war effort and their beloved President Bush. But many also could not help but agree with the brash New Yorker. Jeb had long since lost his place as the front-runner but the latest attack was devastating.

One supporter told CNN at the time that he supported President Bush and the war effort but that he was voting for Trump: "I just don't think we have time and room for another Bush," he said. "I think the country needs a change."

The gamble paid off, of course. Trump beat Marco Rubio and Ted Cruz by 10 points and George W. Bush's little brother, Jeb, quit the primary after losing to Trump by more than 22 points.

The Bush dynasty in the Palmetto State was over.

In the final desperate days of the 2016 election, Hillary Clinton was walking a duplicitous line that was complicated even for a Clinton. She felt she had finally been forgiven by Democrat voters for her vote to invade Iraq. (We would later discover that she probably had not actually been forgiven, since leaked emails show that clearly antiwar Bernie Sanders would have won the nomination in 2016 had the Democrat National Committee not stolen the nomination from him and finally handed it to Clinton.)

Whatever. By the general election, Clinton was calculating to accuse Donald Trump of being a dangerous war-monger who could not be trusted with the nuclear codes. Yet at the same time, Trump himself was arguing that it might not be a bad idea to try getting along with Russia in the mutual interest of killing terrorists.

"What we should do is focus on ISIS. We should not be focusing on Syria," he said in an interview. But he was also acutely aware that at least in voters' eyes, Clinton was still vulnerable for her hotly pro-war record.

"You're going to end up in World War III over Syria if we listen to Hillary Clinton," Trump said.

Moreover, he was acutely aware of the lessons that should have been learned from Korea and Vietnam and, to some extent, Afghanistan. "You're not fighting Syria anymore. You're fighting Syria, Russia, and Iran, all right? Russia is a nuclear country."

Soon enough, Hillary Clinton and deranged Democrat leaders would be accusing Trump of being in bed with Russia and President Vladimir Putin. But for now, they had an election to win so they were claiming the opposite.

As Election Day neared, Clinton and her allies released the most fear-mongering ads since Lyndon B. Johnson. Mushroom clouds, nuclear launch control buttons, the whole works. Anything to get elected.

"The thought of Donald Trump with nuclear weapons scares me to death. It should scare everyone," a former doomsday officer, posing inside a nuclear silo, said in one of the final ads of the campaign. Another ad that ran in Ohio featured a mushroom cloud and the savage remains of Hiroshima. "One nuclear bomb can kill a million people," the narrator intoned. "That's more than all the men, women, and children living in Columbus, Ohio."

The month after that ad, President Trump beat Hillary Clinton in the normally whisker-tight bellwether state of Ohio by more than 8 points, the largest margin in that state since George H. W. Bush beat Michael Dukakis by 11 points for the White House thirty years ago.

Once elected, President Trump rocked the political world by declaring in his inauguration speech that he intended to keep the promises that got him elected. He announced in December 2018 that he plans to pull U.S. troops out of Syria. Republican hawks immediately made their displeasure known. But this should have been no surprise, which Trump himself pointed out.

"Getting out of Syria was no surprise," Trump tweeted about the announcement. "I've been campaigning on it for years, and six months ago, when I very publicly wanted to do it, I agreed to stay longer. Russia, Iran, Syria & others are the local enemy of ISIS. We were doing there [*sic*] work. Time to come home & rebuild. #MAGA." Later, Trump modified his position and has kept enough military advisors on the ground to prevent ISIS from regaining a stronghold in Syria.

What was likely more surprising to those in the political universe was a candidate keeping his campaign promise.

★CHAPTER SEVEN★

ROMNEY'S HOUSE
OF RINO LOSERS

I f you really hate Donald Trump, you are probably not reading this book. You are not among the legions of loony lefties that have hijacked the Democrat Party and dragged it over the cliff of socialism. Nor are you among the small, smug, but incredibly powerful and self-satisfied fat cat Republicans in Washington known as "the Establishment." Also known as "RINOs," which stands for "Republicans In Name Only." The RINOs are a stable of political geldings who call themselves "conservative" and "Republican" but do not actually represent the interests of "conservative" or "Republican" voters around the country.

Instead, they are the passive eunuchs who serve diligently in the court of Democrats. They put up fights from time to time, but always dutifully lose and quietly go back to being loyal eunuchs in the court of Democrat Washington.

Also, if you are reading this book, it is a near certainty that you are not among those afflicted by Donald Trump Derangement Syndrome.

President Trump hugs an American flag at the 2019 Conservative Political Action Conference on March 2, 2019. (Official White House Photo by Tia Dufour)

However, if, by some freak chance, you happen to be among those afflicted with this mentally debilitating disease, then I am here to help you.

If you hate Donald Trump and are looking to place the blame for his election, look no further than Barack Obama and Hillary Clinton. She was arguably the worst possible person Democrats could have nominated in 2016, even if they had legitimately nominated her. We all now know, of course, that the Democrat Party officials actually stole the nomination and rigged the whole process to get Hillary Clinton nominated.

And, in so doing, they did what establishment, power-drunk party elders often do when left to their own dishonest devices to circumvent the will of the people. In Hillary, they picked somebody who was so odious, so patently dishonest, so unlikable that even some dyed-in-the-wool Democrats could not vote for her—in some cases, not even when faced with the choice between her and Donald Trump. In addition to that blizzard of negativity, Hillary Clinton was a has-been retread who had already been roundly rejected by Democrat voters in 2008.

Even if Democrat Party leaders had not rigged the nomination for her, Bernie Sanders would not have beaten Donald Trump. Despite the desires of an increasingly wacky Democrat Party, few Americans are interested in socialism. They know that socialism is an assault on everyday freedoms, that it quashes religion and ultimately kills people—around 100 million over the past one hundred years.

Or, as President Trump said in his 2019 State of the Union address to Congress: "America was founded on liberty and independence—not government coercion, domination, and control. We are born free and we will stay free.

"Tonight," he concluded, "we renew our resolve that America will never be a socialist country."

But the rise of socialist senator Bernie Sanders in the Democrat primary should have been a clear lesson for party leaders that 2016 was setting up to be a major rejection election. The status quo was in peril. Great unrest among voters in both parties meant that the only way to win was with something dramatically new and different.

So, who did the geniuses leading the Democrat Party offer up as an agent of change in this era of clear upheaval?

Hillary Rodham Clinton, who for the past twenty-five years has been trudging around on the national political stage. Her comments covering up her husband's abuse of women—and her toleration and enabling of it—are the fodder of late-night comedians. In the public mind's eye, there she is, hustling in and out of courthouses for depositions, offering faked, icy smiles, and always stuffed into baggy pantsuits, and usually lying about whatever she is talking about.

So here is a woman who owes her entire career to marrying the right man. How on earth was Hillary Clinton ever going to be the face of progressive feminism in an era when so many women in every industry have achieved the highest levels— not because of who they married but because of their hard work, grit, and smarts?

How could Hillary Clinton possibly prosecute the so-called Republican War on Women? How on God's green earth was Hillary Clinton an agent of "change" after twenty-five years in the most powerful posts in national politics and eight years of dismal Democrat rule? Fact is, she had had a strong hand in creating nearly everything that was wrong with the country.

Then, as she hilariously titled her latest book after losing, *What Happened?*

Answer: *You Lost!*

The other Democrat who deserves a huge helping of credit for the rise of Donald Trump is, of course, President Barack Obama. In 2008 he ran a positive and uplifting and unifying campaign. Those promising qualities quickly faded once he settled into the White House.

A LITTLE RETROSPECTIVE

Barack Obama burst onto the national political scene back during the 2004 Democrat convention, where Democrats were doing everything they could to get excited about the thoroughly unexciting John Kerry, who is famously unlikable. He tends to drone on and on and on and—worst of all—he takes himself so seriously when most others don't.

For example, during one campaign stop that year, Kerry thought it would be a really powerful and moving experience for his entourage to visit the hospital in Colorado where he was born. Of course, nobody wanted to see the hospital room where he was born. After all, we're not talking about a manger in Bethlehem. But he dragged an entourage of reporters into the place and tried reenacting the historic moment when he took his first breath and began wailing.

He said something along the lines of "Isn't that hard to imagine." Actually, given all the constant whining reporters had been hearing from him for the better part of a year, it really wasn't hard to imagine.

Needless to say, when the opportunity arose to hear anyone other than John Kerry give a speech, people perked up. And that year, it was Senator Barack Obama. Going back and reading that speech today is enlightening. You get a real sense of why he was such an appealing candidate—even if you did not agree with his brand of politics. He was positive and unifying. You got a real sense that he loved America and cherished the hope and opportunity our country holds.

But it is also illuminating because it reminds you of just how miserably he failed once he tried to govern. You realize what a complete pig-in-the-poke the American people had been sold. He presented himself as an appealing candidate with noble instincts—but then governed as someone entirely different.

In that convention speech, Obama quoted the Founders and celebrated "life, liberty, and the pursuit of happiness." He sounded like a red-blooded American patriot. He expressed gratitude that in America "we can participate in the political process without fear of retribution and that our votes will be counted, at least most of the time."

This is the same man whose administration went on to weaponize the Internal Revenue Service to punish conservatives for their political beliefs. The same administration whose Department of Justice dismissed concerns about members of the New Black Panther Party intimidating voters outside a Philadelphia polling place during the 2008 election.

This is the same administration that fought tooth and nail against efforts to secure voting everywhere to make sure fraudulent voters were not casting votes that would disenfranchise legitimate voters.

And, most chilling of all, this is the same guy whose administration would launch a full-scale spying operation using the government's most powerful domestic espionage apparatus against political opponents at the height of a presidential campaign. And as if that were not terrifying and disgusting enough, officials at the highest levels of the Obama administration collected information on political opponents and leaked that classified information to their toadies in the media in order to punish those enemies.

While we might have been able to "participate in the political process without fear of retribution" before Obama became president, his administration changed that. In that 2004 convention speech, Obama also celebrated individual success. He met people all the time, he said, who "don't expect government to solve all their problems. They know they have to work hard to get ahead—and they want to."

(Until, of course, he got elected four years later. Then, with unparalleled audacity, his message to entrepreneurs became "You didn't build that.")

In the same speech, he warned fellow Democrats that the government was not always the answer: "Go into any inner-city neighborhood and folks will tell you that government alone can't teach our kids to learn—they know that parents have to teach, that children can't achieve unless we raise their expectations and turn off the television sets and eradicate the slander that says a black youth with a book is acting white."

This sounds so promising and heightens the dismay so many felt when he wasted his first two years in office—with control of the House of Representatives and a filibuster-proof majority in the Senate—to ram down Americans' throats an orchestrated takeover by the federal government of the country's health-care industry.

Perhaps the most dishonest part of that famous 2004 speech was where Barack Obama talked about how far Americans had come in terms of racial reconciliation after a long, hard past. "Now even as we speak, there are those who are preparing to divide us, the spin masters, the negative ad peddlers who embrace the politics of anything goes," he said.

"Well, I say to them tonight, there is not a liberal America and a conservative America—there is a United States of America. There is not a black America and a white America and Latino America and Asian America—there is the United States of America."

It was a truly thrilling line. Too bad the evidence shows he didn't mean a word of it.

Needless to say, Obama's legislating days in Washington ended pretty quickly after Democrats jammed through Obamacare. It would be their only significant victory—a victory that set the stage for the calamitous times ahead for the Democrat Party.

Two years later, Democrats would lose the House to the largest Republican majority in history. Obama would also lose six seats in the Senate. Of course, even in the minority, Democrats continued to pursue an unpopular agenda. For Obama's part, he turned to making all sorts of constitutionally questionable administrative changes to jam through the rest of his unpopular agenda.

By the time Obama left office, he and his party had managed to lose more than one thousand seats across the country—along with the majorities in the House and the Senate. But Obama got himself reelected and that was all that mattered to him.

Now Comes Mitt Romney

No matter how looney, stupid, or tone-deaf Democrats in Washington behave, they are forever lucky for the one magical ace they always have up their sleeve: Republicans.

In all fairness, Barack Obama and Hillary Clinton bear the overwhelming burden of responsibility for paving the way for President Trump's ascension into the White House. But a good deal of that responsibility also belongs to Republicans who for years have fielded terrible, spineless candidates, ignored the wishes of their own voters, and made monstrous tactical errors that ultimately brought on their own destruction.

Nobody in the Republican firmament better embodies those suicidal Republican instincts than Mitt Romney, the Great White RINO from Michigan. I mean Boston. Um, no. Actually Utah. Oh, whatever: Willard Mitt Romney is from wherever is most politically expedient at any given moment.

Currently that is Utah, where he now represents the Beehive State in the United States Senate. Because that is the only state where the guy could get elected for a free ride back to Washington.

Now, Romney has been praised as a genius turnaround artist with failing companies. That may be true, but he is also one of the biggest morons at politics to ever run for elected office. It is doubtful the guy could get elected dog catcher from just about any county in the country.

Did someone mention dogs? One of Romney's favorite little homey stories to endear voters to him is about the time he and his family drove a thousand miles in their station wagon. That's nice until you get to the part where they strapped the family dog to the roof and ended up in a car wash because the poor dog had diarrhea.

Yikes. Poor Seamus. Who but a real dope would tell people about something so idiotic? This is a good example of just how tone-deaf Romney is as a candidate.

Good lesson for all future Republican candidates: Americans love their dogs. In fact, they love them far more than they like even the most popular politicians. You are not scoring any points chortling about the time you strapped your family dog to the roof of your car for a vacation a thousand miles away.

But back to Mitt Romney, the politician. Before Mitt Romney was from Utah, he was from Michigan. That is where his father was an auto company executive. George Romney later became governor of Michigan. That is the state from which the elder Romney ran for president, ultimately crashing out of the 1968 campaign after admitting to being "brainwashed" about the war in Vietnam.

After Mitt Romney was from Michigan and before he was from Utah, he was from Boston. It was there—in the liberal land of Ted Kennedy and Elizabeth Warren—that Mitt Romney found his political fortunes.

It is true that when he ran for governor, he ran as a Republican. But he was hardly a Republican in any traditional sense of the word. He was in favor of abortion, against Ronald Reagan, and just fine with illegal immigration—so long as he could get a good deal on yard work. Oh, and so long as it meant cheap labor for all his buddies who owned companies.

And Mitt Romney—speaking I suppose as a man of the people—once memorably remarked during his presidential campaign that he is a huge fan of NASCAR racing. I mean, who isn't, right? Who doesn't like *Talladega Nights* and who hasn't snaked for miles and miles with three coolers of beer to get into Martinsville Speedway to get your eardrums blown out watching cars thunder around the track and plastering you with melted black rubber?

Or, as Romney himself said, tweaking his blue-collar credentials: "I have some great friends who are NASCAR team owners."

Somebody get this guy a stage. He should run for office. Real man of the people!

It was as if there was no setting where Mitt Romney could find himself comfortable among normal people. At a Martin Luther King Day parade in Jacksonville, Florida, for example, he spied a group of people preparing to march. They ranged in age from adults to young children and Romney got excited. He wanted to mingle with them.

So, he jumped out to greet them and said, "Who let the dogs out?"

The group of people, of course, were good sports about it, but they must have wondered what was this white guy talking about. And just when you thought the whole scene could not get more cringe-worthy, Romney announced: "Oh, I see you've got some bling-bling here."

By no means did this suggest in any way that Mitt Romney is racist or even particularly racially insensitive. He was trying his best to connect with people in the warmest, most genuine way he knew possible. But it simply reveals that he doesn't possess the innate skills to do so. Romney still goes to enormous lengths to pander to people and pretend he speaks their language, understands their issues, and wants to represent them.

"Who let the dogs out?"

"Oh, you've got some bling-bling here!"

Lord, please help us.

When it came to actual issues most important to conservatives or Republican voters, Mitt Romney was even more of a clueless caricature of everything voters hate about politicians. On abortion, for example, Romney so terribly contorted himself over the years that by the time he became the Republican nominee for president in 2012, nobody had the earthliest clue where the man actually stood.

A devout Mormon, Romney maintains that he has always been at least personally opposed to abortion. Fine. Good for you. That is not why the question matters to serious people trying to figure out who they are going to vote for. What matters is a politician's view of the law and when life begins and when the constitutionally guaranteed rights to life, liberty, and pursuit of happiness as granted by God kick in for a baby growing in the womb.

When Mitt Romney first ran for the U.S. Senate—during his Massachusetts phase—he adamantly favored abortion: "I believe that abortion should be safe and legal in this country," he said during a debate with Senator Ted Kennedy, in which Romney clearly wanted to be for abortion even more than Kennedy. "I believe that since *Roe v. Wade* has been the law for 20 years it should be sustained and supported," he said. "And I sustain and support that law and support the right of a woman to make that choice."

When he ran for governor in 2002—still in his Massachusetts phase—Romney reiterated his commitment to abortion, saying that he was "devoted and dedicated to honoring my word in that regard."

Luckily for unborn babies everywhere, Romney's word is a pretty fluid thing.

By the time he began positioning to run for president— nearing the end of his Massachusetts phase—Romney completely reversed himself on abortion. He wrote in the conservative magazine *National Review,* "I am pro-life and believe that abortion should be limited to only instances of rape, incest, or to save the life of the mother. I support the reversal of *Roe vs. Wade* because it is bad law and bad medicine."

Roe v. Wade is certainly bad law and bad medicine. But Mitt Romney is an even worse politician. Seriously, think of everyone you know with whom you have discussed the issue of abortion. Can you name a single person who has held this many divergent opinions on a matter of such profound importance and principle?

Back during his 1994 debate with Kennedy, while in his Massachusetts phase, Romney also sought to distance himself from Ronald Reagan and the Gipper's policies, which were dedicated to freedom, prosperity, and personal liberty. Romney would later reverse himself in that area, as well.

Ted Kennedy must have marveled—and maybe quietly envied—the ease with which Mitt Romney could slide from one bedrock principle to the next, depending on the prevailing political necessity of the moment.

It's like the guy never thought anyone kept track of what he said about anything.

For all of the Great White RINO's slipperiness on profoundly important issues of deeply held principle, nothing—and I mean nothing—compared to Romney's unfitness to prosecute the case against Obamacare in 2012.

In the first two years of his administration, Obama bet everything on health care. With control of both chambers of Congress, Obama could have granted amnesty to millions of illegals in the country; he could have passed legislation through Congress to guarantee abortion rights. He could have passed any minimum wage bill he wanted. They could have soaked the rich and raised taxes to kingdom come. He could have legalized gay marriage.

He could have shut down every coal plant in the country and outlawed cars and planes. He could have done, literally, anything he and his big-government acolytes wanted to.

Yet the only thing Democrats really accomplished legislatively during that period was to hijack the nation's health-care system, which the majority of people were perfectly happy with. But it was a way to raise costs for certain people so that the system could pay to cover health care for other people. It was, predictably, hugely unpopular. Democrats would go on for a thousand-seat skid of losing elections around the country before they hit bottom.

The 2012 election was the first and biggest opportunity for Republicans to make Barack Obama himself pay for his hubris, tyrannical tendencies, and terrible governing instincts.

So, who did Republicans pick to carry the battle flag against this monstrosity? They managed to pick the only Republican politician in all of the land who not only failed to oppose Obamacare, but who had actually invented his own version of Obamacare.

Romneycare. Obamneycare. Republican Obamacare. Whatever you want to call it, it would cost Republicans the 2012 election.

Back when Romney was still in his Massachusetts phase and supporting abortion with every fiber of his being, he decided it would be a great idea for the government to take over the state's health-care system to deliver health insurance coverage for everyone.

This sounds nice, but if you are an actual conservative, you understand that governments are abusive by nature and usually the least efficient way to do anything other than the most basic and fundamental tasks. As imperfect as free markets are, they are still the fairest and most efficient way to deliver services such as health insurance. At least that is what most conservatives believe.

That would not be Willard Mitt Romney.

The best Romney could do to confront Obama was to complain not that Obamacare was destroying America's robust health care industry, but only about the manner in which Obama pulled it off.

"I like the fact that in my state, we had Republicans and Democrats come together and work together," Romney fumed during one of the debates with Obama. "What you did instead was to push through a plan without a single Republican vote."

Zing!

Anyway, if there is one thing I have learned covering politics, it's that when Democrats and Republicans emerge from behind closed doors and announce that they have reached a "bipartisan" agreement on something, you had better grab your wallet and run.

But even on this point, the ever-evolving Romney could not hold his fire in the same direction for very long. A few years later, in 2015, after the Staples business supply company founder Tom Stemberg died, Romney recalled how Stemberg encouraged him to think up a plan for Massachusetts to take over health care in the state.

"Without Tom pushing it, I don't think we would have had Romneycare," Romney proudly recalled. "Without

Romneycare, I don't think we would have Obamacare. So, without Tom, a lot of people wouldn't have health insurance."

Except, of course, for those who lost it.

––––––––––––––––––

So, just how did the Republicans end up picking such a loser? The 2012 primary was a murderous affair. Every Republican with a pulse was running: Rudy Giuliani, Rick Santorum, Newt Gingrich, Rick Perry, Herman Cain. Republican voters in every primary state dutifully tried to fall in love with each one of them. Rick, Rudy, Newt!

But for every reason under the sun, each was flawed. All the while, coasting along near the top but never the object of love, was Willard Mitt Romney, the Great White RINO.

At the time, I remember comparing Romney's efforts to get Republican primary voters to fall in love with him—something akin to trying to stuff a cat into a trash can. If you have ever tried this, then you know what a futile effort it is. Not to mention painful.

But, eventually, with inexhaustible persistence, the cat got stuffed into the can. And so Republican primary voters made their choice after trying every last other nominee. In the end, Mitt Romney in 2012 became the Republican Party's John Kerry of 2004 and was dispatched to defeat Barack Obama.

The primary system had created a sort of Frankenstein candidate that checked all the boxes of the mind yet inspired nothing of the heart. And probably stood for nothing to boot. All stripes of Republicans who thought most any candidate could defeat Obama were in for a terrible surprise.

Abandoning bling-bling, Romney pursued a campaign

on behalf of the Republican donor class. The answer to illegal immigration was amnesty. The answer to China was trade. The answer to terrorism was more wars overseas.

On top of everything else, Romney was immensely unlikable. It was as if he believed that the whole concept of conservatism is to crap on the poor—rather than provide a system in which anyone who works hard and plays by the rules can climb to the highest heights of wealth and freedom.

"Forty-seven percent of Americans pay no income tax," Romney groused to a bunch of wealthy donors during a campaign event. "So our message of low taxes doesn't connect," he whined. "[Obama] will be out there talking about tax cuts for the rich. I mean, that's what they sell every four years. And so my job is not to worry about those people. I'll never convince them that they should take personal responsibility for their lives."

Of course, the comments leaked. They were huge news, and they stuck to Romney until the bitter end.

It was the most flaccid, dispiriting prosecution of conservatism in a presidential campaign since, at least, Republican John McCain ran in 2008.

Meanwhile, President Obama was entering Jimmy Carter territory in terms of the stagnating economy and despair across the country.

Clearly, Republicans had fielded a terribly flawed candidate who could not even attack the president on the single most unpopular feature of his first term. Because, actually, the Republican nominee had invented it.

Now Comes Donald Trump

Primary fights almost always make better candidates for the general elections. It is why primaries are always better than brokered conventions. Never has that been truer than it was for Donald Trump in 2016.

It is impossible to overstate just how much credibility Trump built for himself by going after the entire Republican establishment as ferociously as he did right out of the gate in 2015. It was swift. It was personal. It was vicious.

Again and again, Trump showed a raw, jungle-like instinct to find the soft spots in his opponents and home in on them with lion-like savagery. And he did this with cunningly sophisticated tools—as if he had a bank of focus groups advising him. He taunted his adversaries with brutal and flawlessly descriptive names that stuck until the end and beyond. He seemed to get it right every time. And his audiences loved it.

Whether it was illegal immigration or so-called free trade or all the wars around the world, Trump ripped deeply into what had become sacred orthodoxy inside the party that was supposed to be the "conservative" party.

But there is nothing conservative about failing to secure the border. Nor is granting amnesty. Enforcing duly enacted laws with fairness and integrity is perhaps the single most important tenet of conservatism. If the laws are stupid or unnecessary or unduly harsh, overturn them. Otherwise, enforce them. Nothing degrades a society rooted in equal justice under law more than keeping laws on the books that are ignored or unequally enforced.

Nor is there anything conservative about establishing vastly complex international trade agreements where our federal government negotiates with other governments to determine which companies in which industries in which countries win and which ones lose.

Perhaps the least conservative of all the so-called

conservative positions embraced by Republicans in recent decades is the notion of spending trillions and trillions of dollars fixing other people's problems in other parts of the world.

Trump knew the keys to making America great again: build an unmatched military, control the seas that protect us, enforce our borders, and limit foreign military adventurism to unavoidable operations where our national security interests are obvious and pristinely defined.

Unsurprisingly, Republican retreads in Washington like Mitt Romney—now in his Utah phase serving as a U.S. senator—have chafed at President Trump's dismantling of the old, broken GOP agenda they have been driving for so many years. Driving, of course, into the ground.

Few establishment Republicans were stingier toward Trump during the general election than Romney. It was as if he actually wanted Hillary Clinton to win. But for all his caterwauling and complaining, he mainly just showed voters why he lost so miserably in 2012.

Some of Romney's most ardent defenders say that the only reason he lost that election to Barack Obama is that he was wealthy. His idiotic comment about the 47 percent, these people argue, merely reminded people how rich Romney was. What was so disgusting about Romney's 47 percent remark was not that it reminded people that he has money. Rather it revealed his view that nearly half of Americans are a bunch of freeloaders who need to be taken care of.

For actual conservatives, the truly sad thing about welfare is not that society must take care of them. The real tragedy is that these are people who might otherwise be making tremendous contributions to the economy, their communities, and our country as a whole if only the government would quit interfering with the free enterprise system by creating incentives for people not to work.

As for the silly idea that Americans do not like rich people, Donald Trump really put the boot to that. His election proved that Americans actually still like rich people. They just don't like Mitt Romney.

Donald Trump's early entry into Republican primary politics began in Iowa, where he offered kids free rides in his Sikorsky helicopter, the blue one with "Trump" emblazoned down the side. Children loved it. As did their parents. Until Iowa State Fair officials shut it down.

So Trump just moved the whole operation across the street and offered the rides anyway.

The whole glorious scene was a reminder that, yes, Americans still love rich people. They want to be near success. They just don't like fakers and they don't like rich people who look down their noses at them.

Donald Trump is legendary for his brilliant and bombastic instincts. One of my favorite incidents occurred at the Republican convention in Cleveland. Trump's longest-time nemesis, Ted Cruz of Texas, was in a hissy fit and built up plenty of drama leading up to his petty refusal to actually endorse the Republican nominee during the Republican convention.

Displaying the political instincts of a dead clam, Cruz held what could only be described as a campaign rally outside the convention hall to feed the legions of reporters from around the country eager to describe the supposedly deep disunity of the Republican Party. Bleated Cruz: "In an amazing campaign field of seventeen talented, dynamic candidates, we beat fifteen

of those candidates . . . . We just didn't beat sixteen." Then he
looked around, displaying his unctuous Cruz pause.

At that moment, the crowd looked past Ted Cruz and
started booing and pointing skyward. Out of the blue emerged
a plane—a 757 with gold lettering down the side that spelled
"T-R-U-M-P." That moment—and there would be so many like
that—seemed to sum up the formidable mix of brains and
stamina and brashness that took this most unlikely candidate
to the White House.

★CHAPTER EIGHT★

THE STATE OF TRUMP'S UNION

Of all the mistakes people have made about Donald Trump from the time of his arrival on the political stage, none is more fundamental than the effort to stuff him into one of the familiar political molds that dominate the national political power structure. Because everybody in Washington is supposed to fit into one of a handful of proscribed categories, the thinking goes, so must Trump.

Is he a conservative? A Main Street Republican? A Wall Streeter? A progressive Democrat? A war-mongering neoconservative? Maybe some sort of evangelical? Or even a Blue Dog Democrat?

As is now clear, the only mold Donald Trump fits into is his own.

No matter how hard they try, the political pros and pundits have never been able to fit Trump into any one of their preset categories. This is maddening to them. It also leads to a

President Trump delivers State of the Union speech on February 5, 2019.

(Official White House Photo by D. Myles Cullen)

221

monumental misunderstanding of the man and what he seeks to accomplish.

Ironically, understanding Donald Trump and his true motives is much simpler than Washington politicians and the media try to make it. And it has become clear that the wisdom of ordinary Americans allows them to see Trump and his motives much more clearly than traditional political experts do.

From the first moments that Trump emerged on the political scene, it has been clear that he is not a conservative—at least not in the sense that political types think of conservatives. In the first place, conservatives are generally a buttoned-down crowd who don't tend to break much china. The caricature of them might actually be of one delicately holding a china saucer in one hand and a cup in the other hand, little pinky held aloft.

If true conservatives value predictability and order and gradual transitions, count Trump out. He moves with alacrity, disdains exhaustive planning, and is perfectly comfortable taking huge risks. He is the original bull in the china shop.

He called me one time during the primaries when one of his opponents had provoked his special wrath by presenting a complicated flow chart. "A *fourteen-point plan*!?" Trump bellowed over the phone. "Who the hell needs a fourteen-point plan?" Trump asked, incredulous. "Just do something, you know. Who needs a fourteen-point plan? Just fix the problem!"

Fair point, I thought. And perhaps a big reason why I liked Trump from the start. Most fourteen-point plans I had ever seen usually obscured far more than was clarified. They usually seemed to be bureaucratic retreats that just kept the problem alive to be debated another day. For better or for worse, the massive and continuous failure of federal politicians has radicalized me into a bumper sticker man: "Build the Wall."

"Stand Up to China." "Quit the Wars." "Cut Taxes." "Leave Us the Hell Alone!"

The genius of Donald Trump demanding a wall is that every time he does it, he smokes out all the people who really don't want to do anything to fix the wide-open border. If their first reaction to a wall proposal is that a wall will not work, or that we actually need a fence, not a wall, or a wall is immoral, then they probably are not all that serious about securing the border in the first place.

In considering what is at Donald Trump's political core, you can be sure he did not grow up worshipping at the feet of William F. Buckley and reading *National Review*. Nor did he go to Hillsdale College, toy with entering seminary, study exotic religious ethics, and spend a year translating Ayn Rand books into three different languages to spread the word of laissez-faire doctrine.

I know some intelligent people who have done all of these things. Donald Trump just isn't one of them. Perhaps more than anything, he is and always has been a pragmatist. A bombastic pragmatist.

You can see this in his reaction to Obamacare.

As a lifelong, devoted, principled conservative, I am vehemently opposed to Obamacare. I don't want the federal government involved in my health care, period. The government has a terrible record, to begin with. Just look at the Department of Veterans Affairs or bankruptcy-bound Medicare.

But more than that, the notion is appalling that the federal government would have some say in how I get health care, how much I pay for it, and at what point I have to start paying for it out of pocket. As much as I may hate my insurance company, I like the insurance plan I worked out and pay for. And I would rather that those decisions remain between me and my doctor and my insurance company. At least with the insurance company I have some leverage. I can always quit my insurance company and shop somewhere else.

I grew up reading *The Federalist Papers* and early on learned that a federal government that can give you anything—including a morphine drip—can take anything away from you.

Simply put, if the federal government is in charge, you have no leverage. If I want to go to a witch doctor, then, by damn, I ought to be able to. If my insurance company doesn't want to cover my witch doctor, then so be it.

So that is why I and millions of others are against Obamacare.

But that is not why Donald Trump is against Obamacare. He is against Obamacare because it doesn't work. He is not ideological in his stance, and it's not because he hates Democrats or Obama for the viciously partisan way in which the law was passed. Trump hates the policy because it has made a difficult process much more difficult by any commonsense standard.

It's easy to want to kill Obamacare, but President Trump wants to fix it because that's what he does. He sees a problem and talks to people about how to try to fix it. He has conversations with all kinds of people and does what he sees as the best, most concise option. He wants to find practical solutions for problems that trouble regular Americans.

In so many ways, his 2016 presidential campaign and his performance in the White House exemplify that. The campaign was a lean operation that executed the essential needs of a political operation and nothing more. The White House has followed that same model and Trump has been more like a mayor than a typical American president.

But that doesn't mean President Trump is a less powerful or effective leader of conservatism and freedom than past presidents like Ronald Reagan—and the reason is fairly simple. For decades now the entire field of political debate in Washington and among the so-called elites has shifted so far left that political ideas that were part of the radical fringe just a few years ago have become closer to mainstream.

This is largely the result of the relentless work done by three heads of the Leviathan that seeks to destroy the American spirit from the inside: Hollywood, the media, and academia.

On the media, it is important to remember that for a slew of reasons, the press has always leaned leftward. Reporters tend to come from big cities and spend their "learning years" in university settings. And they skew toward being social justice warriors.

Often you hear people lament all the noise of today's chattering media. They pine for "the good old days" when news was confined to the three networks providing a steady diet of seemingly straight news in staid fashion from the likes of Walter Cronkite. As for me, I loved the days when multiple newspapers in major markets came rolling out and were devoured before the pages had time to cool. I cherish my time in Detroit, with two excellent newspapers at each other's throats every day. Yes, even the lore of *The Front Page* suited me just fine. But the truth is, the press was pretty jaded to the left back then, too.

It wasn't until the emergence of talk radio, cable news, and—finally—the Internet that the wool was pulled from America's eyes and people began hearing another side of the "news" as it had been fed to them for forever. The emergence of Fox News as a balance to all the one-sided, monolithic, cosmopolitan drivel has been the greatest example of smart, honest news-gathering aimed at filling the giant void left by the vast, so-called mainstream media.

But giving regular Americans a voice in the national political debate did not come without a price. The result has been the leftward march of once-great institutions like the *New York Times* and the *Washington Post*—papers I grew up reading at home—into partisan hysterics. Both papers have entirely abandoned all pretense of fairness or balance in the Trump era.

Network television news has not done much better. And the liberal cable response to Fox News has been off-the-charts crazy. MSNBC is unwatchable by any fair-minded viewer. CNN, once a respected global cable news-gathering machine, has gone full-throttle looney with seriously impaired anchors and guests whose only requirement seems to be that they are willing to attack Trump. And the political manifestos that crawl along the bottoms of TV screens are not so much informative as they are offensive, taking direct shots at the president of the United States at every moment possible.

During the 2016 campaign, CNN took to using these crawls at the bottom of the screen as real-time "fact checking" opportunities. For example, during the Brett Kavanaugh confirmation process, CNN ran a crawl reading: "White House denies Trump was mocking Kavanaugh accuser after Trump mocks Kavanaugh accuser."

These lower-third banners that are used to ostensibly convey a snapshot of the conversation on the screen have instead been weaponized into another form of editorial opinion woven into the day's "reporting."

As a result of the endlessly dishonest political "journalism" and the general leftward lurch of the media in recent years, the whole field of debate has shifted so far to the left that regular Americans—Republicans, Democrats, and Independents—no longer even recognize the debate.

And the media darlings who are given hours and hours and hours of television time to promote their half-baked political ideas have become kookier and kookier. Few have been kookier than David Corn of *Mother Jones* magazine and Michael Isikoff of the Yahoo! News website. They wrote a book together spinning all the wildest, most unsubstantiated Russian hoax conspiracy theories and titled it, appropriately, *Russian Roulette*. This amuses me, considering who it is that always gets shot when playing Russian roulette.

Even after publicly acknowledging that the nonsense in the so-called Steele Dossier is unsubstantiated and much of it likely false, these two goats, Corn and Isikoff, continued shoveling their slop all over television.

The attention is less on ideas and debate to better the national discourse and more about who can get the best sound bite, go viral, and make a name for themselves in political journalism. The conveying of information to the audience has become almost irrelevant as long as they continue to tune in.

It was precisely that yawning disconnect between the political debate in Washington and the actual concerns among regular Americans that convinced President Trump to run in the first place. "What do these people stand for?" Trump asked with an incredulous half smile on his face one afternoon in his penthouse apartment in the Trump International Hotel in Las Vegas.

It was still early in the primary and the debates still featured nearly two dozen Republicans running for the nomination. As we talked, with the sparkling desert far below, we watched the television. It was muted and showed the debate hall where Trump—polling ahead of everyone else—would take center stage that night with all the other candidates flanking him. Cameras showed different candidates and their campaigns checking out the stage and the podiums. This amused Trump.

"Why can't these people just say what they stand for? Why do they have to go check everything out? I just show up, take center stage, and they line up on either side of me."

He waved the TV away in disgust.

He was wearing a pressed white shirt, open collared, and suit pants. As always, Trump is very comfortable in his own skin. And he genuinely likes talking to people. "All these guys are doing debate prep," he said to me. At this Trump wagged his shoulders back and forth as if mocking a wooden soldier, similar to his waddling presidential duck walk. "I am sitting here with you!" he said. "This is my debate prep right here! Go ahead, ask me some tough questions!" He laughed.

Perhaps the finest display of President Trump's brand of practical conservatism was his State of the Union address in February 2019. It was also the finest speech of his entire political existence. It is important to remember that it was a speech that almost did not happen. The year 2018 ended with the government shut down. President Trump was, of course, being blamed by Democrats, who had just taken control of the House in the 2018 midterms.

Additionally, Democrats were coming into power in the House with the exact same old leadership they had had twelve

years earlier, when they gained control and President George
W. Bush was in the White House. And, as they did the last time
they were in power, Democrats were almost certain to blow
their opportunity by overreaching.

The new Congress had not even begun and Democrats
got right down to the business of overreaching. Of course, the
media blamed President Trump entirely for the shutdown. He
had asked for money to build a wall on the southern border,
something that many Democrats in both the House and the
Senate had favored earlier.

In fact, the wall—or fencing or steel slats or whatever
physical barrier you want to call it—that was being built on
the border at that very moment had been generously supported
by both Democrats and Republicans. But now it was Trump
asking for money to build more barriers. Democrats pounced.
They saw an opportunity to play politics. They refused to give
President Trump any more money for additional walls on the
border. They called him a xenophobic racist.

While the media was blaming President Trump for refusing
to open the federal government unless he got his wall funding,
the reverse was also true. Democrats were suddenly refusing
to fund the government if it meant doing anything more about
securing the southern border. President Trump rightly saw
this as a political opportunity. And while, in the end, President
Trump did not get the funding he wanted before agreeing to
reopen the government, he did manage to win a larger fight.
The master marketer managed to redefine the entire debate
so that it was all about border security and the need to build a
physical barrier at the southern border.

A casualty of the whole shutdown was that after inviting
President Trump to the House chamber to deliver the State

of the Union address, Speaker Nancy Pelosi then withdrew her invitation and canceled the entire event. Ever dishonest and hopelessly terrible at messaging, Pelosi lied and claimed she had to cancel the event for security purposes since the federal government was partially shut down. Only deluded anti-Trumpers, devoted Democrats, and the media failed to see through her idiotic stunt.

Having turned the whole debate about the shutdown into a discussion about how to secure the southern border, and with the ever-important Super Bowl fast approaching, President Trump finally acquiesced to reopen the federal government. Pelosi then reversed herself and once again invited President Trump to come to the House chamber to deliver his second State of the Union address. It would be his best speech yet. It was the finest encapsulation of everything he has stood for and for which his presidency has fought.

The emotional highlight of the speech was, as it has been since President Ronald Reagan began the practice, the heroic American men and women and children President Trump had posted in the gallery for the speech. If it took an acting star from Hollywood to invent the tradition of heroes in the gallery, it was a modern reality television star who perfected it.

The first people President Trump introduced were three heroes from three-quarters of a century ago. Highlighting "the majesty of America's mission and the power for American pride," he introduced Private First Class Joseph Reilly, Staff Sergeant Irving Locker, and Sergeant Herman Zeitchik, who had been among the tens of thousands of American troops who stormed the beaches of Normandy and leapt from Allied airplanes on June 6, 1944, to liberate Europe from the evil grip of Nazi socialism.

It was the simplest celebration of one of America's finest hours. Plenty of people in the chamber that night did not care much for the president, but no one could help but applaud the sacrifice and success of these grizzled old warriors from the Greatest Generation. President Trump would come back to those men and their sacrifices before the night was over.

It was a broadly presidential moment and more than just stylistically. At a time when partisan rancor has never been so deep and harsh in Washington, President Trump sought to find common ground even on political issues that have increasingly divided Americans.

"The agenda I will lay out this evening is not a Republican agenda or a Democrat agenda," he said. "It is the agenda of the American people." Though many of the issues he chose to talk about that night were issues that have led to complete dysfunction and gridlock in Washington, President Trump managed to present them in a way that huge majorities of American citizens would entirely agree with.

There was low-hanging fruit. His declaration of war on childhood cancer included an introduction of ten-year-old Grace Eline, who as a little girl had helped raise forty thousand dollars to fight cancer—only to later be diagnosed with the wretched disease herself.

Also, there was true, genuine bipartisanship, such as his successful efforts to reach across the aisle and find common ground on prison reform. It is certainly not a high priority of political conservatives, but it was a true effort at negotiating with natural political opponents. He talked about his efforts to bring down the cost of drug prices, end human trafficking on the border, and lower unemployment, including among blacks, Hispanics, and women.

On the hottest of hot-button issues in politics today—
abortion—President Trump never flinched. He took possession
of the issue in a manner rarely seen in politics. "Lawmakers
in New York cheered with delight upon passage of legislation
that would allow a baby to be ripped from the mother's womb
moments before birth," he said. "These are living, feeling,
beautiful babies who will never get the chance to share their
love and dreams with the world."

Then he talked about Virginia governor Ralph Northam
and his stunning admission that a law the governor supports
in that state would allow a baby to actually be delivered before
determining with the mother whether to let the child die. But,
the governor said, the baby would be kept "comfortable" while
his or her fate was decided.

Talk about death panels!

With this, the debate is no longer about "pro-choice" versus
"pro-life." It has suddenly become a debate about simple, cold-
blooded murder and is anathema to the millions of American
voters who oppose it. President Trump called on Congress to
"pass legislation to prohibit the late-term abortion of children
who can feel pain in the mother's womb."

In what some felt were the most eloquent words in his
speech, President Trump said, "Let us work together to build
a culture that cherishes innocent life. . . . And let us reaffirm a
fundamental truth: all children—born and unborn—are made
in the holy image of God."

He also spoke of the economic and humanitarian disaster
that has drained the life out of Venezuela over the past decade,
since the once prosperous and thriving country embraced
socialism and turned into "a state of abject poverty and
despair." Like many Americans, President Trump said he was

alarmed by new calls in our own country to adopt socialism. "America was founded on liberty and independence—not government coercion, domination, and control," he said. "We are born free and we will stay free."

Tonight, he said, "we renew our resolve that America will never be a socialist country."

Amazingly, amid the roar of approval, there were actually Democrats in the audience who were sitting on their hands for this. Among them was Vermont senator Bernie Sanders, who sat with a sour-puss look on his face, head shrugged forward like someone had stolen his bicycle. What makes this so shocking—and sad—is that Bernie Sanders is no longer some fringe wacko gadfly nobody listens to, though that is what he has been for most of his political career.

Today Bernie Sanders is one of the most visible and popular leaders of the Democrat Party and he came tantalizingly close to winning the party's nomination for president. In fact, had the primary not been rigged against him and stolen by party leaders and the nomination handed to Hillary Clinton, socialist Bernie Sanders certainly would have been the party's nominee for president in 2016.

This is the political genius of President Trump. Even as he forges common ground with the vast majority of American voters, he also forces his opponents to take increasingly absurd positions. The idea that an avowed socialist holds such a celebrated position of power in a major political party in America today is nothing short of stunning.

As President Trump closed his State of the Union speech, he returned to the old American warriors seated in the balcony of the House chamber. He recalled their sacrifices from so long ago. Then he introduced Joshua Kaufman, an elderly man seated alongside the three American soldiers, Joseph Reilly, Irving Locker, and Herman Zeitchik. The old men exchanged glances and nodded to the crowd.

As a boy, President Trump told the chamber, Joshua Kaufman was a prisoner at the Dachau concentration camp in Poland. As he awaited his destiny in a jammed cattle car, alone and scared, he found a hole in the wall of the car. Looking through the hole, he could see American soldiers and American tanks rolling into the death camp.

"To me," Joshua Kaufman told the world, "those American soldiers were proof that God exists."

Just for a moment, in the magnificent House chamber, we could see America at her shining best and feel again what we can become.

★CHAPTER NINE★

TRUMP 2020—
DOUBLE DOWN

This spring, I sat down with President Trump in the Oval Office and caught up with him about how things were going and how he felt looking toward the 2020 election. It had been nearly four years since we first spoke, when he called me after he read my positive column about his announcement speech.

"That was no notes," he said of his announcement speech, when I reminded him of that first telephone conversation. "I did that sort of spur of the moment."

He smiled and laughed lightly, marveling at his own audacity in announcing a presidential campaign off the cuff. Trump's charm in person is irresistible. That is why all the crazy accusations about him being hateful or racist or evil simply never stick among regular people who are not suffering from Trump Derangement Syndrome.

Before I arrived at the White House, President Trump had hosted Jens Stoltenberg, NATO's secretary-general, to talk about the European Union (EU). When White House spokeswoman

Survivors of a tornado welcome President Trump to Lee County, Alabama in March 2019. (Official White House Photo by Andrea Hanks)

Sarah Sanders ushered me into the Oval Office, the president had retired to his private study to freshen up.

There is always a hushed formality inside the West Wing of the White House. Secret Service agents blend silently into the walls like grandfather clocks. Aides and advisors scurry across the lush carpeting in silence and absolute efficiency. Visitors tend to whisper because they really are not sure where to stand or whether to even speak. Decorum rules everything.

Sarah and I stood waiting for the president, marveling to ourselves at the man's ceaseless energy. We talked about how his unorthodox style and scaldingly honest language has changed the way people talk politics in Washington. So many of the fake niceties have been put away.

Even on an overcast day, a beautiful, slightly filtered light shines through the bank of windows behind his uncluttered desk. Beyond that, the city was glowing in its majestic annual festival of cherry blossoms. On the small table behind his chair are framed black-and-white pictures of his mother and father.

After a few minutes, President Trump came bounding in, wearing a crisp white shirt. Blue suit. Red tie. He had just gargled with Listerine, the classic yellow stuff that scorches the inside of your mouth. He welcomed me and immediately invited me behind the famous Resolute Desk for a picture.

For the longest time after Trump first began running for president, I studiously avoided riding on his plane or being in any situation where I might be unavoidably invited into a picture with him. Part of that is just the automatic reflexes of a reporter who never wants to be too chummy with somebody he is covering, either as straight reporter or as an opinion columnist. I never wanted anybody to doubt the sincerity of my opinions about the guy.

But I also never wanted Trump to have some embarrassing picture of me standing beside him smiling, thumbs up, for the camera in the event he abandoned his campaign promises, in which case I would have readily turned harshly against him.

That never happened. So I happily walked around for a picture with him. I might have even offered a smile and a thumbs-up.

When we sat down, Sarah Sanders and I took two chairs opposite him across his desk. He spoke graciously about how much he appreciates my routinely defending him in my columns for the *Washington Times* and in television appearances on Fox News.

"You're tough," he says. "I like that."

Then he looked at Sarah and an impish grin crossed his face. He told me I could have all the time I needed in this interview. Then he added, "Don't let Sarah push you around."

We all laughed, because it was genuinely funny. But like bear cubs play-fighting, there was something more serious going on. He was testing a little. Did I have the spine to blow her off if she—being the excellent press secretary that she is—started rushing me to finish my interview so he could get to more important presidential business?

Among confident people it is an easy test. But it also would have revealed any weakness. And Trump—ever watching—would have recorded it.

Of course, Donald Trump certainly likes to test people. He says something and watches your face for a reaction. He is always pushing, looking for those soft spots in people. And the hard spines that do not budge. He can be belittling, but also highly complimentary.

When not testing people, Trump likes to review his record—

whether it is his accomplishments, his epic public fights, or the slights people have committed against him. In this case, he wanted to linger a little longer on his announcement speech back in June 2015.

"You know, it's funny," he said. "They gave me great marks for a great speech.

"And then, about three days later, remember?" he asks. "It was like a delay. They said, did he use the word 'rape'?"

He was talking, obviously, about his line about the Mexican rapists that caused such a firestorm.

"Okay, so I did," he confessed. "You know, the 'rape' word you don't use. But I used it."

It really doesn't matter how many millions of times the media has chewed this over, Trump talks about it with great interest and vigor—as if it just happened yesterday and he is talking about it for the first time.

Now, he said, we have had a couple of years to evaluate his comment about rapists illegally crossing the border into the United States.

"Okay, now we have a few years behind us, right? But the only thing I was wrong about: that it was *mild* compared to what is going on," he said, drawing out the word "mild."

"That speech was tame by comparison to what is happening."

He said he was astonished when he learned from Border Patrol agents that mothers were giving their young daughters birth control pills before their treks north across the border so that they would not become pregnant if they were raped along the way.

Whether you love Trump or hate him, you have to admit that the guy has stuck with the issues that got him elected like a dog with a bone. That is not to say he has successfully solved all the problems he vowed to fix. Illegal immigration is a good example. Even as the problem has gotten worse, Trump has redoubled and redoubled his efforts to solve the crisis at the border once and for all—in the face of constant opposition from Democrats and even some Republicans in Congress.

During the first two years of his presidency, as Trump has remained unswervingly focused on the issues that got him elected, Democrats in Congress have been focused on something entirely different. Instead of debating Trump about the issues, Democrats have painstakingly woven a ludicrous web of lies about some supposed "collusion" between Donald Trump's 2016 presidential campaign and Russia.

Anyone who was following Trump's campaign knew that the campaign had a hard enough time colluding with itself on most day-to-day matters. The idea that they were colluding with a foreign government that speaks a different language was laughable on the spot. But, of course, the media took every bit of it totally seriously—hook, line, and sinker. And they ran with it, clucking ceaselessly like so many Chicken Littles.

Imagine what must have been going through President Trump's mind the first time he heard all the lurid, disgusting, and entirely fabricated claims contained in the so-called Steele Dossier, which we now know was nothing but a crude political hit job. These claims were shared directly with him by his top U.S. intelligence officials.

I asked Trump what has been the lowest, hardest moments of his presidency. When he dismissed the question several times, I could not tell if he simply did not think it mattered or did not care to dwell on anything that hinted of weakness on his part.

Finally, he answered, sort of.

"The biggest moments are when I found out how totally dishonest the press is," Trump said. "Where a story should have been good on the Russia delusion—you know, the whole thing with Russia—and it would end up being horrible."

He looked over to Sarah, adding, "Sarah knows it better than anybody." She smiled and nodded.

Given the madness of the entire Russia "collusion" investigation, I asked how close he came to firing special prosecutor Bob Mueller.

"I never came close to firing him," Trump said.

Why?

"I am a student of history in a true sense," he said. "Certainly, I watched what happened to Richard Nixon when he fired everybody. That didn't work out too well. So, I didn't."

For anyone who actually cares about the Constitution and relies on our free press to hold government officials accountable, these are incredibly frustrating times. While most of the media has been on a two-year drunken bender over their phantom Russia "collusion" crusade, they have entirely missed the very real and far more important story.

Under Barack Obama's previous administration, America's intelligence services were turned over to political partisans who spied on domestic political enemies and used the product of that illegal domestic espionage to punish their political enemies.

This actually happened. In America. In 2016. And, yet, if you were a devoted consumer of most of the media in America the past two years, you very well may have never heard a word about it.

The notion that an administration would spy on political enemies at the height of a presidential campaign is absolutely terrifying. It is the sort of thing that happens in North Korea or Russia. Not in a constitutional republic.

Even more terrifying is that you have a supposedly free press that has almost entirely ignored the scandal. And we are talking about a scandal that is way worse than Watergate and every bit as bad as the Pentagon Papers. And hardly a peep out of the press.

At least President Trump is clear-eyed about the seriousness of the true constitutional crisis, however ignored it may be by the press. "This is something that should never be allowed to happen to another president," he told me.

And it was not just the spying on his campaign during the election that raises seriously alarming questions. All the hyperpartisan actions inside the Department of Justice that we now know about should horrify any red-blooded American, no matter their partisan stripe.

Rogue agents inside the FBI were lustily pursuing a political candidate whom they clearly loathed. All the while, you had the same agents working overtime to squelch a legitimate investigation into another political candidate, Hillary Clinton, whom they clearly favored and fully expected to become the next president—and their next ultimate boss.

This level of clandestine corruption at the highest levels of the federal government is supposed to be why good reporters become reporters in the first place. It is the kind of story we dream about uncovering. Yet, for the vast majority of Washington political reporters, it was virtually ignored.

"I don't think it was ever like this," President Trump said. "I don't think that there has ever been a time—whether it's politics or not—like the corruption [that's been] uncovered.

"Hopefully that's going to be pursued," he added, almost wistfully. "By reporters, too."

Few people come in for a greater beating in this whole scandal than former FBI director Jim Comey, who was one of the top ringleaders of the Russia charade.

"I think Comey was a poor man's J. Edgar Hoover," said Trump, referring to the corrupt former FBI director who collected dirt on political figures so that he could control them. "What he did with that [Steele Dossier] report, I think, was [an effort] to sort of gain influence over the president of the United States."

Then he offered an incredulous smile.

"It didn't work out too good for him," Trump said, citing his refusal to be intimidated by the lurid and outlandish accusations. "It worked out because I had the opposite reaction.

"But Hoover made a living off doing that for many years," Trump added. "He was there for many, many years."

Trump then came about as close as he ever does to chiding or correcting himself.

"I didn't see it at the time," he said with a half shrug. "But, in retrospect, that had something to do with what was happening."

Even in this, however, President Trump takes pride.

"You know, it's very interesting. A lot of things have been exposed in my administration that never would have been exposed in a more typical administration," he said of the FBI's clear vendetta against him, exposed in the aftermath of Comey's firing.

"I am very proud of it. Now you can keep your guard up, at least. You can do what you have to do.

"It is amazing that I won in light of what we found out," he added.

"When you talk about collusion, the collusion is with Google and Facebook and all of these different platforms— all of these different companies—with the Democrats. And beyond those, it's the *New York Times,* the *Washington Post.*"

Then, shifting back to the big picture, he said, "So, I've done a lot of good. I think I've done more than anybody in the first two years ever as president, if you really think about it."

He paused a moment, looked past me to the open door.

"Hey," he called out. "Give me the list of things!"

Turning back to me, he said excitedly, "I just wrote out a list." Copies of the long list of his administration's accomplishments were brought in and passed around.

"It goes on for pages, okay? *Pages!*" Three single-spaced pages, to be exact.

The list chronicles all the details of the booming economy, rising wages, and falling unemployment that have occurred during Trump's first two years in office.

"Look what I just did for Israel two days ago," he said, referring to his declaration to recognize the Israeli-occupied Golan Heights as sovereign property of Israel.

"They've been talking about that for forty-eight years, right? I did it in two seconds," he said with a wave of his hand.

Throughout Donald J. Trump's short, triumphant political career, he has been truly blessed with the greatest gift every politician prays for: terrible opponents. Whether it is Jeb Bush or Hillary Clinton, Trump's opponents have been, to use a favorite term of Trump's, "real beauties."

Looking toward 2020, those beauties get more and more beautiful every day. He is looking at everything from fake Indians to fired porn star lawyers to open-border fanatics. The most sensible among them are the full-blown socialists.

If Donald Trump's 2016 election was the barbarians storming the gates of Washington, this Democrat field looks more like the lunatics trying to take over the asylum. The first debate will look like a scene from *One Flew Over the Cuckoo's Nest,* with one of them barking, another refusing to take his meds, and another screeching across the white floor without pants.

Meanwhile, on planet earth, President Trump will be the character played by Jack Nicholson, utterly pole-axed by the sheer lunacy of the entire bunch, but also thoroughly enjoying it and taking every opportunity to offer encouragement for each one to flaunt their zaniest ideas.

Trump can barely conceal his glee over the opportunity to face such a bunch in the election. "We have three hundred fifty million people living in America and this is the best we can do?" he asks, smiling.

Always nearby the Oval Office is Dan Scavino, the president's director of social media, a clear nod to how important Trump thinks it is to communicate directly to voters instead of going through the traditional media outlets.

While we were talking, Scavino walked into Trump's office with blown-up copies of a fresh tweet, hot off Scavino's printer. It was from Jens Stoltenberg, the NATO secretary-general, who had just been meeting with Trump moments before I arrived.

Scavino handed out copies of the printed tweet to President Trump, Sarah, and me. It was three minutes old. Trump's eyes flitted over the printed page, then he showed a small smile.

"Great discussion with President Trump," Trump read approvingly.

In his tweet, Mr. Stoltenberg thanked Trump for "keeping #NATO strong."

"His message on fairer burden sharing is having a real impact," Stoltenberg wrote. "By the end of next year, European Allies & Canada will have added $100 [billion] to their defense spending."

President Trump smiled and looked up. "You think that's good?"

To the very end, President Trump seems unafraid to tackle any topic or issue. Unlike the vast majority of politicians, he is not governed by the slightest hint of political correctness.

"What's going to happen with the Smollett case?" he asked me, inquiring about the horrendous episode in Chicago where police charged black actor Jussie Smollett with setting up an elaborate hoax in which he paid two African brothers to beat him up so that he could blame a couple of guys in Make America Great Again (MAGA) hats and claim it was a racially motivated hate crime.

Trump said that indeed it was a "hate crime," but it was a "hate crime" committed against his supporters.

"That's a hate crime," he said. "He blamed that on MAGA. He said MAGA did that."

Trump is clearly incensed over the smearing of his supporters. "Those are great people," he said firmly. "Great people.

"They had the lawyer of the two brothers on last night. He said they put whiteface on," Trump continued. "It's incredible how dishonest the whole thing is. But that's a hate crime. A hate crime is a federal situation. And you know, [Smollett] was anti-MAGA before."

The whole situation has been terrible for Chicago, he said.

"Chicago is a great city. Hey, look, I have a big tower in Chicago. Now [Chicago's] being scoffed at all over the world."

The city's mayor, Rahm Emanuel, who blamed the hoax on the political tone set by Donald Trump, bears some of the responsibility, Trump said.

"Rahm has turned out to be a horrible mayor. He looked like such a fool," Trump said.

After a pause, he added, "You know, his brother is a good friend of mine. Ari. And, uh, I spoke to him two days ago."

Trump chuckled, before continuing, "He's embarrassed by the whole thing.

"Rahm has turned out to be such a terrible mayor," he repeated. "I wouldn't have thought it was possible."

Trump shrugged.

Nothing animates the president more than when he talks about his supporters and how horribly they get maligned by the media. It is why he prefers to talk directly to them, instead of trying to trust the political press to accurately convey his messages to them.

"You know, you almost know your enemies when they start saying, 'Don't use Twitter, don't use Twitter.'

"I had a beautiful woman in Ohio a few weeks ago," he smiled.

"'Please, please don't give up Twitter. Please! Please! It is so important,'" he quoted the beautiful woman in Ohio as telling him.

He called out for Scavino again, asking for the very latest totals on the number of followers he has across all the social media platforms that he controls: 168 million followers, according to Scavino's latest tally.

I joked that he was going to put me out of business.

His charm reflex kicked in.

"You'll never be out of business," he said. "You're the best guy around."

I was reminded again of our first conversation nearly four years earlier. Trump is always complimentary of people, especially people who are complimentary of him. He likes people who like him. This is, probably, the single most common trait found among all politicians in all of history. It's why he is so energized by the massive rallies with thousands of ordinary Americans who, unlike so many Washington wonks, love him for just who he is.

The people who matter to President Trump—and the whole reason I endorsed him the day he announced and have pretty much stuck up for him ever since—are the regular working Americans for whom he speaks.

I asked him how he handles all the constant, vicious, and often dishonest vitriol directed at him. He waved it off like it doesn't really matter but acknowledged, "Nobody's ever had to do this."

And then he answered, "I always say, 'Do I have a choice? You know, really, do I have a choice?'

"A lot of guys would have sat in the corner, put their thumb in their mouth, and said, 'Mommy, take me home.' It's true."

I asked why he doesn't just give it all up and walk away, go back to his very full and enjoyable life of luxury.

"I couldn't do that," he says flatly.

"I would never do that. I just couldn't do that.

"I really feel an obligation," he said earnestly. "You know, we have millions of people out there that are counting on me. I really feel that strongly."

My Endorsement of Donald Trump
from June 16, 2015

DONALD TRUMP DECLARES WAR ON LYING, STREET-HUSTLERS OF CONGRESS

BY CHARLES HURT

THE WASHINGTON TIMES, JUNE 16, 2015

ANALYSIS/OPINION:

Finally, a serious and truly experienced contender. Donald Trump and his $9 billion just made the biggest splash of the 2016 presidential race.

By the time the seas stop sloshing back and forth, there may not be a drop of water left over for anybody else to float a rowboat.

Of course, what you heard from Washington and the elite political set in both parties Tuesday was snickering and laughing and scoffing. All the old jokes about the Donald's cheesy style. His crazy orange comb-over. His penchant for grand statements spoken bluntly with an exclamation point that is often dotted by his very own finger in the air.

And, yes, he descended down to his kickoff at Trump Towers via a glass escalator. It was shopping mall glamorous.

As presidential announcements go, it was brilliant. It was simple, and it was patriotic.

No sun-splashed park with throngs of rented people jammed around an H-shaped stage. No fake columns.

Just a stage and a velvet blue curtain and a podium. Flanked by American flags carefully folded to show both stars and stripes, Mr. Trump wore a simple uniform of red tie, white shirt, blue suit. Red, white, and blue.

Get it? Red, white, and blue? America's colors? The flag? In other words, Mr. Trump loves America. Get it?

It sounds so simple, yet it is so terribly complicated for all the geniuses around here who get paid monstrous amounts of money by political campaigns to put on events like this. They get into earth tones and pantsuits and open-collared shirts.

You can imagine Mr. Trump shaking his head, patience drained, just before he fires somebody.

"No! I want American flags behind me," you can hear him saying in an exasperated tone. "I want a red tie, white shirt, and blue suit. Get it?

Red, white, and blue? I love America and I want to return her to greatness so I am going to wear red, white, and blue."

Then came Mr. Trump's take on what is wrong with America today. It was a scalding evisceration of politicians in both parties and all their terrible ideas and lazy neglect of fierce and festering problems.

He shredded them for everything from trade to defense to unemployment to immigration. And "the disaster called 'The Big Lie.' Obamacare!"

And in one sentence, he shone a light on the only path anyone should have ever used to combat Obamacare: It is A LIE! The president and his party are liars and they lie every time they tell people that the government will make people's lives better. It is a complete lie just to shake down people for more money and accumulate more power for themselves. It is a scam. Total street hustler scam and Obamacare is the biggest of them all.

If the president and his party are telling the truth about all the wonderful ways government can make your life so much better, why is there rioting in Missouri and Baltimore and California after *six years* of Obama and Democrat rule? Why are so many people so desperately miserable today?

"We don't have victories," Mr. Trump said, before running through all the foreign countries that beat America all the time in trade, immigration, defense, and economy.

"I beat China all the time," he said flatly. "All the time.

"When was the last time you saw a Chevrolet in Tokyo? It doesn't exist."

Mr. Trump then turned southward.

"When do we beat Mexico?" he asked. "At the border, they are laughing at us—at our stupidity. They are not our friend, but they are killing us economically."

Who talks like this? Name one single politician today in either party who is this plainly articulate. Unafraid to say precisely what we are all thinking.

"The U.S. has become a dumping ground for everybody else's problems," he said.

Donald Trump is the Godzilla we all wanted Sarah Palin to be. He is the real renegade. He is the businessman we wanted Mitt Romney to be. He is the straight-talker that George W. Bush was on good days.

Another way you know that Mr. Trump is manna from heaven for America is to hear all the clowns in media and politics who were perfectly horrified by the spectacle of Mr. Trump's announcement.

Look no further than the simpering and insufferable *Washington Post,* which is the very face of everything that is wrong with political insiderism and incestuous journalism today.

"Terrible," the flailing paper declared of Mr. Trump's candidacy. Why?

"People like Marco Rubio, Jeb Bush, Scott Walker, Mike Huckabee and everyone else on that debate stage will be playing by one set of rules, Trump will be playing by another. Or, more accurately: Trump won't be playing by any rules."

Dear God, help us. America is falling to pieces. Russia, China, and Iran are plotting to destroy us. Radical Islamists want to slit every one of our throats. And the best these idiots can come up with is Hillary Clinton. And what they are worried about are the rules of some stupid debate nobody's gonna watch.

We really are ruined—at least until this current crowd of liars, fakers, and frauds are tossed aside. At least Donald Trump understands that much.

★

ACKNOWLEDGMENTS

S incere thanks to my editor, Kate Hartson, and her terrific team at Hachette Books for their encouragement and assistance in helping me publish this book. My thanks as well as to my literary agents, Matt Latimer and Keith Urbahn, of Javelin. Matt is a great friend who is endlessly creative and always generous with his creativity. This book would not have been done without him.

Fox News has been a rare shining light the past three years, covering the rise of President Trump honestly and fairly, refusing to get sucked into the blind anti-Trump hysteria that has seized so much of the media. Chris Stirewalt—one of my oldest friends in Washington—Tucker Carlson, Bill Sammon, Bret Baier, and so many others at Fox are not only great colleagues but also wonderful friends in a town where true friends are usually only of the canine variety.

Speaking of which, deep thanks also goes to Molly, Harper, and Hickory, who are great friends and also actual dogs. Their approving looks and patient attention keep me relatively sane working in a city teetering on the edge of madness.

It goes without saying, but probably should be said anyway, that eternal gratitude goes to my long-suffering wife, Stephanie, and our three extraordinary children, Lily, Henry, and Sam. They make everything in life worth it.

No one has been more patient and encouraging than the *Washington Times*, whose careful balance during these turbulent political times should be a lesson for all newspapers. In particular, Chris Dolan, Larry Beasley, and Stephen Dinan are some of the best and most honest news guys around.

Finally, my greatest thanks goes to my father, Henry Hurt, who is the best, truest and most fearless reporter I have ever known. A brilliant writer, he is also a great editor—both of words and in life. For a million reasons, this book would not exist if not for him.

—Charles Hurt
Tightsqueeze, Virginia
May 1, 2019

INDEX

A

Abortion(s)/abortion rights
  back alley/coat hanger,
    136–37
  constitutional protection,
    132–33
  late-term, 232
  Planned Parenthood v. Casey
    and, 141–42
  pro-choice/pro-life, 31, 208
  Roe v. Wade and, 133–34,
    141–44, 207–08
  Romney and, 205, 207–09
  Trump view on, 232
  underage children, 145
affirmative action/racial quotas,
  149–50
Afghanistan, 175, 178, 188–89,
  192
African American(s). *See also*
  police/law enforcement;
  racism; racist (label)
  Black Lives Matter
    movement, 93–94
  civil rights movement, 86–87
  "Hands Up, Don't Shoot" and
    "Ferguson Effect," 91–94
  hate crimes towards, 249
  identity politics and, 33–34
  judicial nominations, 143–46

  Trump outreach to, 58, 231
  voter suppression, 89–90
Alito, Samuel, 140, 157
alternative reality/facts, 6
alt-right (racist label), 97, 99
American flag, 17, 27, 256–57
American populism, 6
The Apprentice (TV show), 65
Arctic National Wildlife Refuge
  (ANWR), 71–73
Asian(s), 33, 186, 203

B

Baldwin, Alex, 119
Baltimore, MD, 18, 91, 93, 257
Bannon, Steve, 45–46
Barry, Maryanne Trump, 159
Becoming (Obama), 41–42
Benghazi attack, 187–88
bipartisanship, 12, 67, 179, 210,
  231. *See also* partisan politics
birther claims, 5–6, 35, 38–39,
  41–42
Black Lives Matter movement,
  93–94
Blackmun, Harry, 141–42
border wall, 222–23, 229
Bork, Robert, 134–38
Brennan, William, 140
Breyer, Stephen, 142

263

ABOUT THE AUTHOR

CHARLES HURT is a reporter and political commentator. He is currently the opinion editor of *The Washington Times* and a contributor to Fox News. Previously, he was an editor at Drudge Report and the *New York Post*'s D.C. bureau chief covering Washington politics.